CASSEROLES

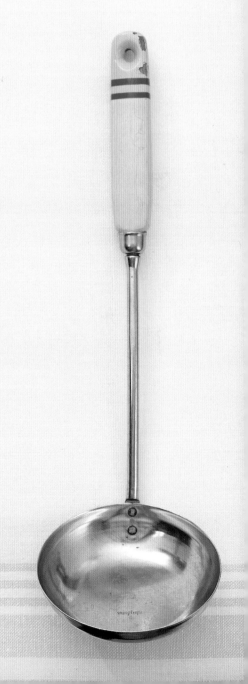

Introduction

Casseroles should feature in every cook's repertoire.
These steaming one pot wonders always go down a treat,
whether traditional classics or brimming with exciting new
flavours. Amazingly, some of our recipes take less than
30 minutes to cook, and to give you a head start on a busy
week, we've lots of ideas for preparing and freezing ahead.

Every recipe has been triple-tested to ensure perfect
results, and if you should find yourself missing that
all-important piece of cookware, visit the home of creative
kitchenware at www.lakeland.co.uk. You're sure to find just
what you're looking for, from dependable basics such as
foil and baking parchment, to equipment that will serve
you well through many years of cookery to come.

LAKELAND

This book was created for Lakeland by ACP Books
Copyright © ACP Magazines Ltd 2008

ISBN: 978-1-903777-26-8

Printed and bound in China

contents

tips & techniques

Casseroles are among the simplest of dishes. Once you've put the dish on to cook, your work is done – time and heat take care of the rest. It's the long, slow cooking that brings out the flavours and makes the meat succulent and tender. There are a few things you need to know, though, before you put your feet up.

slow cooker

As a guide, recipes where long, slow oven or cook-top cooking is specified are suitable for a slow cooker.

■ Before you begin, it is important to read the manufacturer's instructions thoroughly. Always follow all safety precautions given in the booklet.

■ Refer to the recipe booklet provided by the manufacturer to work out the cooking time for the recipes you select from this book. Always cover a slow cooker with its lid; do not lift the lid too often during cooking in order to maintain heat.

■ Slow cookers do not allow food to reach a high temperature; the food is meant to be cooked over a long period of time – up to about 8 hours.

■ Coating the meat in flour and browning it before adding it to the slow cooker helps keep the meat tender and locks in the juices of the meat.

■ If your casserole has too much liquid, turn the slow cooker onto the highest setting and cook, uncovered, until some of the liquid has evaporated.

pressure cooker

Many of our recipes can be adapted to cook in a pressure cooker. A recipe is not suitable for pressure cooking when the casserole cooks in about 30 to 40 minutes.

freezing

Unless they contain fish, dairy products, or are mainly made up of vegetables, casseroles can be frozen successfully.

■ It is important to cool the food quickly in the refrigerator before freezing. According to guidelines, hot food should be covered, then placed directly in the refrigerator to cool. Modern refrigerators can cope with the load. Place the hot dish on a heatproof tray to protect the refrigerator shelf.

■ Remove and discard any fat then spoon casserole into a freezer container, leaving about 3cm (1in) at the top for expansion, or line a bowl with a plastic bag, spoon in the cooled casserole and freeze. Once the casserole is frozen, lift plastic bag out of the bowl and squeeze out any air, sealing with a tie.

■ Choose containers that will protect the food from other flavours and odours. They should also be easy to seal and easy to label.

■ Casseroles can be frozen up to 2 months.

■ Thaw casserole in refrigerator overnight before reheating. Add green vegetables and dairy products just before serving.

■ Check the consistency as flour-thickened sauces sometimes break down when frozen and you may need to re-thicken the casserole by adding a little extra blended flour and water, then stirring until mixture boils.

■ Before you begin, it is important to thoroughly read the manufacturer's instructions. Always follow all safety precautions.

■ You may need to refer to the manufacturer's recipe booklet to work out the cooking time for the recipes you select from this book.

■ Cut the meat into even-sized pieces to ensure even cooking.

■ Recipes with a high liquid content usually work best for pressure cookers.

■ You should never fill the pressure cooker more than two-thirds full.

■ As a rule, cooking time is reduced to about a third. For example, a casserole cooked for 1 hour in the oven could be expected to cook in about 20 minutes in a pressure cooker.

■ Thicken with cornflour, etc., and add herbs and green vegetables after the meat or chicken is tender, or just before serving. Simply remove the lid and use the pressure cooker like a saucepan.

cookware

Casserole cookware is available in a large variety of shapes, sizes and finishes. Some casserole dishes are only ovenproof, while others are flameproof.

■ Ovenproof dishes can be used in the oven without breaking; these include earthenware, china, glass and some types of clay pottery.

■ Flameproof dishes can be used in the oven as well as on the cook-top; these include cast iron and stainless steel dishes. Cast iron dishes retain higher heat than most other cookware, so cooking time and temperature may need to be reduced slightly. Where we have used a cast iron dish we have called it a 'flameproof casserole dish'.

■ Ensure cookware lids are tight-fitting when food is cooked covered, or cover tightly with foil.

■ The shape of the cookware doesn't matter. Size does, however: if cookware is too small the food may boil over, too large and the food may dry out.

microwave

We haven't tested any of these recipes in the microwave, but there are many parts of these recipes that would be suitable for microwave cooking. Most casseroles can be cooked in the microwave oven, but we prefer the longer, slower cooking methods.

■ It's important to follow the manufacturer's instructions when using your microwave, and always follow all safety precautions.

■ A combination of convection and microwave cooking will give good results.

cooking your casserole

Follow this advice and make every casserole a fuss-free feast. From choosing the correct meat to preparation and cooking, these guidelines ensure the best results every time.

choosing ingredients

Marbled meat, perfect for casseroles

Slow cooking in liquid tenderises even the toughest meat, so the cheaper cuts are suitable for casseroles. In fact, it's best to avoid the more expensive cuts, as they tend to be lean, and can become dry. Meat that is well marbled, or streaked with internal fat, is best; the fat melts after an hour or so in the dish, making the meat beautifully succulent. If you're making a beef casserole, look for chuck or round steak or gravy beef; if you're cooking lamb, buy chump chops or lamb shanks; if it's chicken, use drumsticks or thighs.
Root vegetables are the ones most often used in casseroles – they're strongly flavoured and their starch content can help to thicken the sauce. Happily, they are usually the cheaper vegetables. But don't make the mistake of buying vegetables past their prime; fresh is always best, even with long, slow cooking. Old vegetables, as well as lacking nutrition, will not contribute much to the flavour of a casserole.

preparing the meat

Trim away any surplus fat from the meat first. The weights given in our recipes take this wastage into account. When cutting meat, cut across the grain. Conversely, when cutting a chicken thigh fillet, cut lengthways with the grain. This helps the chicken to keep its shape and produces a more tender dish.

flouring and browning

The first stage of the cooking process often involves coating the meat with flour and browning it in butter and/or oil. This process gives the meat a coating that seals in the flavour and juices. The flour also thickens the liquid during cooking, while browning imparts a good rich colour to the casserole.
Toss the meat in the flour just before browning. Don't do this ahead of time because the meat juices will absorb the flour and the coating will become gluey. You can put the meat in a bowl, turning the pieces in flour by hand, or throw everything in a clean plastic bag, toss it and shake off the excess flour.

Coating meat with flour in bowl

Heat butter and/or oil in a heavy-base saucepan or flameproof casserole dish and add the floured meat, in batches. Sear the meat quickly over medium to high heat, turning the pieces until they are golden brown and sealed on all sides. Always be careful not to crowd the pan. If you try to cook too many pieces at once, they will stew rather than brown.

cooking

Our recipes give you the approximate litre capacity for cookware. The shape doesn't matter, however, if cookware is too small, food may boil over, and if too large, food may dry out. Flameproof dishes can be used in the oven as well as on the stove-top — these include cast-iron and stainless-steel dishes. Cast-iron dishes retain higher heat than most other cookware, so cooking time and temperature may need to be reduced slightly. To prevent sauce sticking, ensure the dish has a heavy base and a close-fitting lid, or is covered tightly with foil. Use a simmer mat on a gas burner, so the flame can be dispersed evenly and kept low.

As a rule, cooking time in the oven will be longer than on the stove-top. Simply continue to cook until meat is tender when pierced with a fork, or follow guidelines in the recipe. Many of these recipes can be adapted to cook in slow cookers or pressure cookers (see page 4). The success of a casserole depends on long, slow simmering. Once the dish has been brought to a boil, reduce heat and simmer gently. If the liquid boils for an extended period, meat can become tough and dry.

Browning meat in casserole dish

Adding stock to simmering casserole

make now, eat later

Casseroles are excellent do-ahead dishes. They don't suffer at all for being stored in the fridge for a day or two. In fact, many casseroles are much tastier after being left a while, as the flavours have had a chance to develop. You can also remove the fat when the casserole is cold, making it a much healthier dish.

Cook the casserole a day in advance and cool as quickly as possible. Hot food should be covered, then placed directly in the refrigerator to cool: modern refrigerators can cope with the load but you should place the hot dish on a heatproof tray at first to protect the shelf. Just before reheating, remove any fat that has solidified on top.

cuts of meat

These cuts are good to use in slow cookers and pressure cookers.

Beef
chuck steak
beef skirt
blade steak
diced beef minced beef
round steak
thin flank

Lamb
diced lamb
neck chops
shanks

Veal
diced veal
shanks
shoulder

Chicken
diced chicken
drumsticks
leg joints
thigh joints
thigh fillets
whole chicken
wings

Pork
belly
diced pork
leg steak
neck end
rump
shoulder

beef

beef & prune tagine

PREPARATION TIME 20 MINUTES   COOKING TIME 2 HOURS 30 MINUTES

2 LARGE RED ONIONS (600g), CHOPPED FINELY
2 TABLESPOONS OLIVE OIL
1 TEASPOON CRACKED BLACK PEPPER
PINCH SAFFRON THREADS
1 TEASPOON GROUND CINNAMON
1/4 TEASPOON GROUND GINGER
1kg BEEF BLADE STEAK, DICED INTO 4cm (1½in) PIECES
50g BUTTER, CHOPPED
425g CAN DICED TOMATOES
250ml WATER
2 TABLESPOONS WHITE SUGAR
100g TOASTED SLIVERED ALMONDS
250g STONED PRUNES
1 TEASPOON FINELY GRATED LEMON RIND
1/4 TEASPOON GROUND CINNAMON, EXTRA

1   Combine onion, oil, pepper, saffron, cinnamon and ginger in large bowl, add beef; toss beef to coat in mixture.
2   Place beef in large deep saucepan with butter, undrained tomatoes, the water, half of the sugar and 65g of the nuts; bring to a boil. Reduce heat; simmer, covered, 1½ hours. Remove 250ml cooking liquid; reserve. Simmer tagine, uncovered, 30 minutes. (Can be frozen after this stage.)
3   Meanwhile, place prunes in small bowl, cover with boiling water; stand 20 minutes, drain. Place prunes in small saucepan with rind, extra cinnamon, remaining sugar and reserved cooking liquid; bring to a boil. Reduce heat; simmer, uncovered, about 15 minutes or until prunes soften. Stir into tagine.
4   Sprinkle tagine with remaining nuts and serve with spinach couscous (see page 88).

SERVES 4
PER SERVING (INCL. COUSCOUS) 50.3g FAT; 4799KJ (1148 CAL)

TAGINES Interestingly enough, a tagine actually cooks by steaming, just like your microwave oven. With its circular shallow base and tall coned lid, a tagine is the unglazed clay container used to make this traditional Moroccan stew. When the steam rises to the top of the conical lid, it condenses and drips or slides back down into the food in continuous cycle. Serve tagines accompanied by steamed couscous with plumped raisins and finely chopped fresh coriander tossed into it at the last moment.

beef bourguignon

PREPARATION TIME 25 MINUTES COOKING TIME 2 HOURS 30 MINUTES

1kg BEEF CHUCK STEAK
2 TABLESPOONS VEGETABLE OIL
60g BUTTER
10 BABY ONIONS (250g)
400g BUTTON MUSHROOMS
3 BACON RASHERS (210g), CHOPPED COARSELY
1 CLOVE GARLIC, CRUSHED
35g PLAIN FLOUR
250ml BEEF STOCK
250ml DRY RED WINE
2 BAY LEAVES
1 TABLESPOON BROWN SUGAR
3 TEASPOONS FINELY CHOPPED FRESH OREGANO

1 Cut beef into 3cm (1in) pieces. Heat half of the oil in large saucepan; cook beef, in batches, until browned. Remove from pan.
2 Heat remaining oil and butter in pan; cook onions, mushrooms, bacon and garlic, stirring, until onions are browned lightly. Stir in flour; stir over heat until mixture is browned.
3 Remove from heat. Gradually stir in stock and wine; stir over heat until sauce boils and thickens.
4 Return beef and any juices to pan; add bay leaves, sugar and oregano. Simmer, covered, about 2 hours or until beef is tender, stirring occasionally. Discard bay leaves.

SERVES 4
PER SERVING 36.3g FAT; 2890KJ (690 CAL)

classic beef casserole

2 TABLESPOONS VEGETABLE OIL
2kg BEEF CHUCK STEAK, CHOPPED
COARSELY
2 MEDIUM BROWN ONIONS (300g),
SLICED THINLY
2 MEDIUM CARROTS (240g), SLICED
THICKLY
3 CLOVES GARLIC, CRUSHED
3 TABLESPOONS FINELY CHOPPED
FRESH PARSLEY
70g TOMATO PASTE
2 TEASPOONS FRENCH MUSTARD
250ml DRY RED WINE
125ml BEEF STOCK

PREPARATION TIME 15 MINUTES   COOKING TIME 2 HOURS
15 MINUTES

1   Heat oil in 2.5 litre flameproof casserole dish; cook beef, in
batches, until browned. Remove from dish.
2   Add onion, carrot and garlic to dish; cook, stirring, until onion is soft.
3   Return beef to dish; stir in parsley, paste, mustard, wine and stock.
Cook, covered, in slow oven about 1¾ hours or until beef is tender.

SERVES 6
PER SERVING 23g FAT; 2318KJ (554 CAL)

STORAGE Recipe can
be made a day ahead and
refrigerated, covered. Recipe
suitable for freezing.

beef stew with parsley dumplings

1kg BEEF CHUCK STEAK, DICED
INTO 5cm (2in) PIECES
2 TABLESPOONS PLAIN FLOUR
2 TABLESPOONS OLIVE OIL
20g BUTTER
2 MEDIUM BROWN ONIONS (300g),
CHOPPED COARSELY
2 CLOVES GARLIC, CRUSHED
2 MEDIUM CARROTS (240g),
CHOPPED COARSELY
250ml DRY RED WINE
2 TABLESPOONS TOMATO PASTE
500ml BEEF STOCK
4 SPRIGS FRESH THYME

PARSLEY DUMPLINGS
150g SELF-RAISING FLOUR
50g BUTTER
1 EGG, BEATEN LIGHTLY
20g COARSELY GRATED PARMESAN
CHEESE
3 TABLESPOONS FINELY CHOPPED
FRESH FLAT-LEAF PARSLEY
50g DRAINED SUN-DRIED
TOMATOES, CHOPPED FINELY
60ml MILK

PREPARATION TIME 20 MINUTES COOKING TIME 2 HOURS 30 MINUTES

1 Preheat oven to moderate.
2 Coat beef in flour; shake off excess. Heat oil in large flameproof casserole dish; cook beef, in batches, until browned all over.
3 Melt butter in same dish; cook onion, garlic and carrot, stirring, until vegetables soften. Add wine; cook, stirring, until liquid reduces to 65ml. Return beef to dish with paste, stock and thyme; bring to a boil. Cover; cook in moderate oven 1¾ hours.
4 Meanwhile, make parsley dumpling mixture.
5 Remove dish from oven; uncover. Drop level tablespoons of the dumpling mixture, about 2cm (¾in) apart, onto top of stew. Cook, uncovered, in moderate oven about 20 minutes or until dumplings are browned lightly and cooked through. Serve with a mixed green salad dressed with vinaigrette.

PARSLEY DUMPLINGS Place flour in medium bowl; rub in butter. Stir in egg, cheese, parsley, tomato and enough milk to make a soft, sticky dough.

SERVES 4
PER SERVING 39.7g FAT; 3457KJ (827 CAL)

oxtail stew

PREPARATION TIME 25 MINUTES
COOKING TIME 2 HOURS

2kg COARSELY CHOPPED OXTAIL
PLAIN FLOUR
60g GHEE
2 LARGE BROWN ONIONS (400g),
SLICED THINLY
2 CLOVES GARLIC, CRUSHED
2 TEASPOONS COARSELY CHOPPED
FRESH ROSEMARY
60ml DRY RED WINE
2 LARGE PARSNIPS (360g), SLICED THICKLY
2 MEDIUM CARROTS (240g), SLICED THICKLY
750ml BEEF STOCK
I TEASPOON FRESHLY GROUND
BLACK PEPPER
2 MEDIUM COURGETTES (240g), SLICED
THICKLY
250ml TOMATO PUREE
I TABLESPOON COARSELY CHOPPED
FRESH PARSLEY

1   Toss oxtail in flour; shake away
excess flour. Heat ghee in large pan;
cook oxtail, in batches, stirring, until well
browned all over. Drain on kitchen paper.
2   Add onion, garlic and rosemary to
pan; cook, stirring, until onion is soft.
3   Add wine; cook, stirring, until liquid
reduces by a half.
4   Return oxtail to pan; add parsnip,
carrot, stock and pepper. Cook, covered,
1¼ hours.
5   Add courgettes, tomato puree and
parsley; cook, uncovered, 20 minutes or
until oxtail is tender.

SERVES 6
PER SERVING 68.8g FAT; 3664KJ
(875 CAL)

STORAGE Recipe best made a
day ahead and refrigerated, covered. Recipe suitable for freezing.

beef hot pot

STORAGE Recipe can be made a day ahead and refrigerated, covered. Recipe suitable for freezing.

White sweet potatoes, available from ethnic markets and stores, have a creamy-white flesh, unlike the more familiar orange-fleshed variety.

PREPARATION TIME 30 MINUTES
COOKING TIME 2 HOURS 30 MINUTES

2kg BEEF CHUCK STEAK, CHOPPED COARSELY
PLAIN FLOUR
60ml VEGETABLE OIL
2 LARGE BROWN ONIONS (400g), CHOPPED FINELY
4 BACON RASHERS (285g), CHOPPED COARSELY
1 LITRE BEEF STOCK
1 SMALL SWEET POTATO (250g), CHOPPED COARSELY
200g WHITE SWEET POTATOES, CHOPPED COARSELY
4 BABY NEW POTATOES (160g)
2 TABLESPOONS COARSELY CHOPPED FRESH THYME
1 TABLESPOON TOMATO PASTE
1 TABLESPOON FINELY CHOPPED FRESH PARSLEY

1 Toss beef in flour; shake away excess flour. Heat half of the oil in 2.5 litre flameproof casserole dish; cook onion and bacon, stirring, until onion is soft. Remove from dish.
2 Heat remaining oil in dish; cook beef, in batches, until browned. Return onion mixture to dish; stir in stock. Cook, covered, in moderate oven 1 hour.
3 Add sweet potatoes, potatoes and thyme. Cook, covered, 1 hour or until beef is tender.
4 Stir in tomato paste; serve sprinkled with parsley.

SERVES 8
PER SERVING 20.5g FAT; 2064KJ (493 CAL)

osso buco

PREPARATION TIME 30 MINUTES   COOKING TIME 2 HOURS 45 MINUTES

12 PIECES VEAL OSSO BUCO (3kg)
35g PLAIN FLOUR
60ml OLIVE OIL
40g BUTTER
1 MEDIUM BROWN ONION (150g), CHOPPED COARSELY
2 CLOVES GARLIC, CHOPPED FINELY
3 TRIMMED CELERY STALKS (300g), CHOPPED COARSELY
2 LARGE CARROTS (360g), CHOPPED COARSELY
4 MEDIUM TOMATOES (600g), CHOPPED COARSELY
2 TABLESPOONS TOMATO PASTE
250ml DRY WHITE WINE
250ml BEEF STOCK
400g CAN CRUSHED TOMATOES
4 SPRIGS FRESH LEMON THYME
75g DRAINED SEMI-DRIED TOMATOES
60ml LEMON JUICE
1 TABLESPOON FINELY GRATED LEMON RIND
75g PITTED KALAMATA OLIVES

GREMOLATA
1 TABLESPOON FINELY GRATED LEMON RIND
4 TABLESPOONS FINELY CHOPPED FRESH FLAT-LEAF PARSLEY
2 CLOVES GARLIC, CHOPPED FINELY

GREMOLATA is the garnish traditionally strewn over a classic osso buco in Italian cooking just before serving. The scent of its combined ingredients excite the palate once they hit the heat. Nowadays, it's made from any number of aromatic ingredients and sprinkled over many different dishes, from soups to steamed vegetables. For a twist on the more usual version, use orange instead of lemon rind.

1   Coat veal in flour; shake off excess. Heat oil in large deep saucepan; cook veal, in batches, until browned all over.
2   Melt butter in same pan; cook onion, garlic, celery and carrot, stirring, until vegetables just soften. Stir in fresh tomato, paste, wine, stock, undrained tomatoes and thyme. Return veal to pan, fitting pieces upright and tightly together in single layer; bring to a boil. Reduce heat; simmer, covered, 1¾ hours. Stir in semi-dried tomatoes; simmer, uncovered, about 30 minutes or until veal is tender. (Suitable for freezing after this stage.)
3   Combine ingredients for gremolata in small bowl. Remove veal from pan; cover to keep warm. Bring sauce to a boil; boil, uncovered, about 10 minutes or until sauce thickens slightly. Stir in juice, rind and olives. Divide veal among serving plates; top with sauce, sprinkle with gremolata.
4   Serve with soft polenta (see page 87).

SERVES 6
PER SERVING (INCL. POLENTA)   22.4g FAT; 3357KJ (803 CAL)

beef, barley & mushroom stew

PREPARATION TIME 35 MINUTES   COOKING TIME 2 HOURS 20 MINUTES

1kg BEEF CHUCK STEAK, DICED
INTO 3cm (1in) PIECES
35g PLAIN FLOUR
2 TABLESPOONS OLIVE OIL
20g BUTTER
2 MEDIUM BROWN ONIONS (300g),
CHOPPED FINELY
3 CLOVES GARLIC, CRUSHED
1 MEDIUM CARROT (120g),
CHOPPED FINELY
1 TRIMMED CELERY STALK (100g),
CHOPPED FINELY
4 SPRIGS FRESH THYME
1 SPRIG FRESH ROSEMARY
1 BAY LEAF
100g PEARL BARLEY
500ml BEEF STOCK
125ml DRY WHITE WINE
500ml WATER
200g SWISS BROWN MUSHROOMS,
QUARTERED
200g BUTTON MUSHROOMS,
QUARTERED

1   Preheat oven to moderately low.
2   Coat beef in flour; shake off excess. Heat oil in large flameproof casserole dish; cook beef, in batches, until browned all over.
3   Melt butter in same dish; cook onion, garlic, carrot, celery and herbs, stirring, until vegetables soften. Add barley, stock, wine and the water; bring to a boil. Return beef to dish, cover; cook in moderately low oven 1½ hours.
4   Stir in mushrooms; cook, uncovered, in moderately slow oven about 30 minutes or until beef and mushrooms are tender.
5   Serve stew with parsnip mash (see page 86), sprinkled with fresh thyme, if desired.

SERVES 4
PER SERVING (INCL. MASH) 35.1g FAT; 3390KJ (811 CAL)

TIP Pearl barley, the most common form of barley, has had the husk removed, then been hulled and polished so that only the 'pearl' of the original grain remains, much the same as white rice.

STORAGE Recipe suitable for freezing.

TIP If possible, get your butcher to dice the veal shoulder for you.

STORAGE Recipe suitable for freezing.

veal with red wine & balsamic vinegar

60ml OLIVE OIL
1kg DICED VEAL SHOULDER
10 PICKLING ONIONS (400g), HALVED
1 MEDIUM CARROT (120g), CHOPPED FINELY
1 TRIMMED CELERY STALK (100g), CHOPPED FINELY
2 CLOVES GARLIC, CHOPPED FINELY
4 BACON RASHERS (280g), RIND REMOVED, CHOPPED COARSELY
60ml BALSAMIC VINEGAR
2 TABLESPOONS TOMATO PASTE
200g MUSHROOMS, QUARTERED
425g CAN DICED TOMATOES
250ml DRY RED WINE
250ml BEEF STOCK
2 TABLESPOONS COARSELY CHOPPED FRESH GARLIC CHIVES

PREPARATION TIME 25 MINUTES COOKING TIME 2 HOURS

1 Preheat oven to moderately low.
2 Heat 2 tablespoons of the oil in large flameproof casserole dish; cook veal, in batches, until browned all over.
3 Heat remaining oil in same dish; cook onion, carrot, celery, garlic and bacon, stirring, until vegetables soften. Add vinegar and paste; cook, uncovered, 2 minutes.
4 Add mushrooms, undrained tomatoes, wine and stock; bring to a boil. Boil, uncovered, 5 minutes. Return veal to dish, cover; cook in moderately slow oven about 1½ hours or until veal is tender. Stir in chives.
5 Serve veal with creamy garlic mash (see page 86).

SERVES 4
PER SERVING (INCL. MASH) 25.5g FAT; 2495KJ (597 CAL)

beef

cuban shredded beef

PREPARATION TIME 40 MINUTES
COOKING TIME 2 HOURS 50 MINUTES

2 LITRES WATER
1 BAY LEAF
5 CLOVES GARLIC, QUARTERED
6 BLACK PEPPERCORNS
1 LARGE CARROT (180g), CHOPPED COARSELY
1 TRIMMED CELERY STALK (100g), CHOPPED COARSELY
1.5kg BEEF SKIRT STEAK
2 TEASPOONS DRIED OREGANO
1 TABLESPOON OLIVE OIL
1 MEDIUM RED PEPPER (200g), SLICED THICKLY
1 MEDIUM GREEN PEPPER (200g), SLICED THICKLY
2 MEDIUM BROWN ONIONS (300g), SLICED THICKLY
400g CAN WHOLE TOMATOES
1 TEASPOON GROUND CUMIN
150g PIMIENTO-STUFFED GREEN OLIVES, HALVED
60ml LEMON JUICE

SOFRITO
1 TABLESPOON OLIVE OIL
2 BACON RASHERS (140g), RIND REMOVED, CHOPPED FINELY
3 CLOVES GARLIC, CRUSHED
1 SMALL BROWN ONION (80g), CHOPPED FINELY
1/2 SMALL GREEN PEPPER (75g), CHOPPED FINELY
1 TABLESPOON TOMATO PASTE
2 TABLESPOONS RED WINE VINEGAR

1 Combine the water, bay leaf, garlic, peppercorns, carrot, celery, beef and 1 teaspoon of the oregano in large deep saucepan; bring to a boil. Reduce heat; simmer, uncovered, about 2 hours or until beef is tender.
2 Meanwhile, make sofrito.
3 Remove beef from braising liquid. Strain liquid over large bowl; discard solids. Using two forks, shred beef coarsely. (Suitable for freezing after this stage.)
4 Heat oil in same cleaned pan; cook sofrito, peppers and onion, stirring, until vegetables soften. Return beef and braising liquid to pan with undrained tomatoes, cumin and remaining oregano; bring to a boil. Reduce heat; simmer, uncovered, 20 minutes. Remove from heat; stir in olives and juice.
5 Serve shredded beef with spanish rice and peas (see page 89).

SOFRITO Heat oil in small frying pan; cook bacon, garlic, onion and pepper, stirring, until onions soften. Add paste and vinegar; cook, stirring, until vinegar evaporates. Cool 10 minutes; blend or process until smooth.

SERVES 6
PER SERVING 25.8g FAT; 3177KJ (760 CAL)

chilli con carne

PREPARATION TIME 25 MINUTES **COOKING TIME** 1 HOUR 30 MINUTES

1kg BEEF CHUCK STEAK
2 TABLESPOONS OLIVE OIL
2 MEDIUM BROWN ONIONS (300g), CHOPPED FINELY
3 CLOVES GARLIC, CRUSHED
3 TEASPOONS GROUND CUMIN
1 TEASPOON GROUND CORIANDER
1 TEASPOON CHILLI POWDER
1 TABLESPOON FINELY CHOPPED FRESH OREGANO
2 X 425g CANS TOMATOES
250ml BEEF STOCK
2 TEASPOONS BROWN SUGAR
310g CAN RED KIDNEY BEANS, RINSED, DRAINED

1 Cut beef into 2cm (¾in) pieces. Heat half of the oil in large pan; cook beef, in batches, until browned. Drain on kitchen paper.
2 Heat remaining oil in pan; cook onion, garlic, spices and oregano, stirring, until onion is soft.
3 Add undrained crushed tomatoes, stock, sugar and beef; simmer, covered, about 1 hour or until beef is tender.
4 Stir beans into beef mixture; simmer 5 minutes or until heated through.

SERVES 6
PER SERVING 14.9g FAT; 1484KJ (354 CAL)

STORAGE Recipe can be made a day ahead and refrigerated, covered. Recipe suitable for freezing.

TIPS A tortilla (pronounced tor-tee-yah) is a pliable, very thin unleavened bread that originated in Mexico and is still the bread product eaten daily by Hispanics every-where. Tortillas are made either of wheat flour or ground corn meal, and can be purchased fresh, frozen or vacuum-packed.

STORAGE Recipe suitable for freezing.

mexican beans & sausages

PREPARATION TIME 20 MINUTES (PLUS STANDING TIME)
COOKING TIME 2 HOURS 15 MINUTES

200g DRIED KIDNEY BEANS
800g BEEF SAUSAGES, CHOPPED COARSELY
1 TABLESPOON OLIVE OIL
1 LARGE WHITE ONION (200g), CHOPPED COARSELY
3 CLOVES GARLIC, CRUSHED
1 LARGE RED PEPPER (350g), CHOPPED COARSELY
1/2 TEASPOON GROUND CUMIN
2 TEASPOONS SWEET SMOKED PAPRIKA
1 TEASPOON DRIED CHILLI FLAKES
2 X 400g CANS CRUSHED TOMATOES
2 TABLESPOONS COARSELY CHOPPED FRESH OREGANO

1 Place beans in medium bowl, cover with cold water; stand over-night, drain. Rinse under cold water; drain. Place beans in medium saucepan of boiling water; return to a boil. Reduce heat; simmer, uncovered, about 30 minutes or until beans are almost tender. Drain.
2 Cook sausages, in batches, in large deep saucepan until browned; drain on absorbent paper.
3 Heat oil in same pan; cook onion, garlic and capsicum, stirring, until onion softens. Add cumin, paprika and chilli; cook, stirring, about 2 minutes or until fragrant. Add beans and undrained tomatoes; bring to a boil. Reduce heat; simmer, covered, about 1 hour or until beans are tender. Return sausages to pan; simmer, covered, about 10 minutes or until sausages are cooked through. Remove from heat; stir in oregano.
4 Serve with tortillas, if desired.

SERVES 4
PER SERVING 56.9g FAT; 3323KJ (795 CAL)

lamb

rogan josh

2 TEASPOONS GROUND
CARDAMOM
2 TEASPOONS GROUND CUMIN
2 TEASPOONS GROUND
CORIANDER
1kg BONED LEG OF LAMB, TRIMMED,
DICED INTO 3cm (1in) PIECES
20g BUTTER
2 TABLESPOONS VEGETABLE OIL
2 MEDIUM BROWN ONIONS (300g),
SLICED THINLY
4cm (1½in) PIECE FRESH GINGER
(20g), GRATED
4 CLOVES GARLIC, CRUSHED
2 TEASPOONS SWEET PAPRIKA
½ TEASPOON CAYENNE PEPPER
125ml BEEF STOCK
425g CAN CRUSHED TOMATOES
2 BAY LEAVES
2 CINNAMON STICKS
200g PLAIN YOGURT
110g TOASTED SLIVERED ALMONDS
1 FRESH LONG RED CHILLI, SLICED
THINLY

PREPARATION TIME 20 MINUTES   COOKING TIME 2 HOURS

1   Combine cardamom, cumin and coriander in medium bowl, add lamb; toss lamb to coat in spice mixture.
2   Heat butter and half of the oil in large deep saucepan; cook lamb, in batches, until browned all over.
3   Heat remaining oil in same pan; cook onion, ginger, garlic, paprika and cayenne over low heat, stirring, until onion softens.
4   Return lamb to pan with stock, undrained tomatoes, bay leaves and cinnamon. Add yogurt, 1 tablespoon at a time, stirring well between each addition; bring to a boil. Reduce heat; simmer, covered, about 1½ hours or until lamb is tender.
5   Sprinkle lamb with nuts and chilli off the heat; serve with cucumber raita (see page 90) and, if desired, warmed naan bread.

SERVES 4
PER SERVING (INCL. RAITA)   48.1g FAT; 3219KJ (770 CAL)

TIPS A variety of ready-to-eat Indian breads are available in supermarkets, specialty food shops and delicatessens.
■ Naan, a leavened bread, is traditionally cooked against the inside wall of a tandoor, a brick oven. A thick, doughy bread, it is usually served with tandoor-cooked chicken or fish.
■ Unleavened breads, generically called roti, include chapati, puri and paratha, and are used to scoop up pieces of food in lieu of cutlery.

STORAGE Recipe suitable for freezing.

irish stew

60ml VEGETABLE OIL
2kg LAMB NECK CHOPS
1 MEDIUM LEEK (350g), CHOPPED FINELY
3 LARGE POTATOES (900g), CHOPPED COARSELY
2 MEDIUM CARROTS (240g), CHOPPED COARSELY
1 TABLESPOON FINELY CHOPPED FRESH THYME
1 LITRE LAMB OR CHICKEN STOCK

PREPARATION TIME 15 MINUTES COOKING TIME 1 HOUR 20 MINUTES

1 Heat half of the oil in large saucepan; cook chops, in batches, until browned lightly all over. Remove from pan.
2 Heat remaining oil in pan; cook leek, stirring, until just tender.
3 Add potato, carrot and thyme, then return chops to pan with stock; simmer, covered, about 1 hour or until chops are tender.

SERVES 8
PER SERVING 22.1g FAT; 1929KJ (461 CAL)

braised lamb shanks
with sun-dried tomatoes

3kg LARGE LAMB SHANKS
PLAIN FLOUR
2 TABLESPOONS OLIVE OIL
12 BABY ONIONS (300g)
55g DRAINED SUN-DRIED
TOMATOES
125ml PORT
375ml DRY RED WINE
125ml CHICKEN STOCK
2 TABLESPOONS FINELY CHOPPED
FRESH PARSLEY

PREPARATION TIME 15 MINUTES COOKING TIME 2 HOURS
30 MINUTES

1 Toss lamb in flour; shake away excess flour. Heat oil in large
baking dish; cook lamb, in batches, until browned all over. Drain on
absorbent paper.
2 Return lamb to dish; add onions, tomatoes, port, wine and stock.
Cover; cook in moderate oven about 2 hours or until lamb is tender.
3 Remove lamb from dish; keep warm. Simmer pan juices over heat
until thickened slightly.
4 Serve lamb with pan juices; sprinkle with parsley.

SERVES 8
PER SERVING 25g FAT; 1832KJ (438 CAL)

STORAGE Recipe can
be made a day ahead and
refrigerated, covered. Recipe
suitable for freezing.

STORAGE Recipe can be made a day ahead and refrigerated, covered. Recipe suitable for freezing; thicken with cornflour just before serving.

lamb pot roast

PREPARATION TIME 20 MINUTES (PLUS MARINATING TIME)
COOKING TIME 2 HOURS

The casserole dish for a pot roast should be heavy with a well-fitting lid. Good quality pans with a thick, heavy base will hold and distribute heat evenly. If the dish is flameproof as well as ovenproof, it is even more useful. Ideal cuts of meat for pot-roasting include rolled shoulder, trimmed roasts or a forequarter roast.

2 X 1kg BONED ROLLED LAMB SHOULDERS
2 CLOVES GARLIC, CRUSHED
2 FRESH ROSEMARY SPRIGS
1 TEASPOON COARSELY CHOPPED FRESH THYME
1 TEASPOON GRATED ORANGE RIND
250ml DRY RED WINE
1 TEASPOON OLIVE OIL
4 BACON RASHERS (285g), CHOPPED COARSELY
370g SPRING ONIONS, TRIMMED
1 TABLESPOON CHICKEN STOCK POWDER
12 BABY NEW POTATOES (480g)
2 MEDIUM CARROTS (240g), HALVED
2 TEASPOONS CORNFLOUR
1 TABLESPOON WATER

1   Combine lamb, garlic, herbs, rind and wine in large bowl; cover, refrigerate several hours or overnight.
2   Remove lamb from marinade; reserve marinade. Pat lamb dry with absorbent paper; brush with oil.
3   Heat 3 litre deep, flameproof casserole dish; cook lamb until browned all over. Remove from dish. Add bacon and onion to dish; cook, stirring, until onion is browned lightly.
4   Return lamb to dish. Add reserved marinade and stock powder; cook, covered in moderate oven 45 minutes.
5   Add potatoes and carrot; cook, covered, about 1 hour or until lamb and vegetables are tender. Remove lamb and vegetables from dish.
6   Discard all but 500ml of the cooking liquid. Add blended cornflour and water to dish. Stir in cooking liquid; stir over heat until mixture boils and thickens slightly.
7   Serve sliced lamb and vegetables with sauce.

SERVES 8
PER SERVING   16.7g FAT; 1858KJ (444 CAL)

lamb & artichoke stew

3 MEDIUM GLOBE ARTICHOKES (800g)
60ml LEMON JUICE
60ml OLIVE OIL
1 LARGE BROWN ONION (200g),
SLICED THINLY
1.5kg DICED LAMB
PLAIN FLOUR
625ml CHICKEN STOCK
1 TEASPOON GRATED LEMON RIND
2 MEDIUM CARROTS (240g),
SLICED THICKLY
150g FROZEN BROAD BEANS,
THAWED, PEELED
1 TABLESPOON TOMATO PASTE
1 TABLESPOON COARSELY
CHOPPED FRESH DILL
125g PITTED BLACK OLIVES

PREPARATION TIME 30 MINUTES   COOKING TIME 1 HOUR
35 MINUTES

1   Remove tough outer leaves from artichokes; trim tips of
remaining leaves with scissors. Cut artichokes in half; place
artichokes and juice in large saucepan of boiling water. Simmer,
uncovered, about 25 minutes or until tender; drain.
2   Meanwhile, heat 1 tablespoon of the oil in small saucepan; cook
onion, stirring, until soft. Remove from pan.
3   Toss lamb in flour; shake away excess flour. Heat remaining oil
in pan; cook lamb, in batches, until browned.
4   Return onion to pan with stock and rind; simmer, uncovered,
45 minutes, stirring occasionally.
5   Add carrots; simmer, uncovered, 10 minutes. Add beans and
artichokes; simmer, uncovered, 15 minutes or until lamb and
vegetables are tender.
6   Stir in paste, dill and olives.

SERVES 6
PER SERVING 19.2g FAT; 1986KJ (474 CAL)

STORAGE Recipe can
be made a day ahead and
refrigerated, covered. Recipe
suitable for freezing.

lancashire hot pot

8 LAMB NECK CHOPS (1kg)
3 MEDIUM BROWN ONIONS
(450g), SLICED THINLY
3 LARGE POTATOES (900g),
SLICED THINLY
4 BACON RASHERS (285g),
CHOPPED FINELY
430ml BEEF STOCK
30g BUTTER, CHOPPED
COARSELY

PREPARATION TIME 15 MINUTES   COOKING TIME 3 HOURS

1   Trim fat from chops; place chops in 3 litre ovenproof casserole dish. Top with a layer of onion, potato and bacon. Repeat layering, ending with potatoes. Pour over stock; top with butter.
2   Cook, covered, in moderately slow oven 2 hours. Remove cover; cook about 1 hour or until chops are tender.
3   Serve with baby carrots, if desired.

SERVES 4
PER SERVING 24.4g FAT; 2537KJ (606 CAL)

lamb

lamb & okra in rich tomato sauce with garlic confit

PREPARATION TIME 20 MINUTES   COOKING TIME 2 HOURS 10 MINUTES

1 TABLESPOON OLIVE OIL
1kg BONED LAMB SHOULDER, TRIMMED, CHOPPED COARSELY
2 MEDIUM BROWN ONIONS (300g), CHOPPED COARSELY
7 MEDIUM TOMATOES (1kg), CHOPPED COARSELY
1 LITRE WATER
200g OKRA
30g LOOSELY PACKED FRESH MINT LEAVES

GARLIC CONFIT
1 TEASPOON CORIANDER SEEDS
1/2 TEASPOON CARDAMOM SEEDS
30g BUTTER
5 CLOVES GARLIC, SLICED THINLY
1 TEASPOON DRIED CHILLI FLAKES
1 TEASPOON SALT

1 Heat oil in large deep saucepan; cook lamb, in batches, until browned all over.
2 Cook onion in same pan, stirring, until soft. Add tomato and the water; bring to a boil. Return lamb to pan, reduce heat; simmer, uncovered, stirring occasionally, about 1 3/4 hours or until lamb is tender.
3 Add okra to lamb mixture; simmer, uncovered, about 15 minutes or until okra is tender.
4 Meanwhile, make garlic confit.
5 Serve casserole with garlic confit, mint and steamed long-grain white rice, if desired.

GARLIC CONFIT Using mortar and pestle, crush seeds. Melt butter in small saucepan; cook seeds, garlic, chilli and salt over low heat, stirring, about 10 minutes or until garlic softens.

SERVES 4
PER SERVING 33.5g FAT; 2286KJ (547 CAL)

CONFIT is a preserved food item, usually a meat like duck, goose or pork. Salted and cooked slowly in its own fat, the meat is then packed into a ceramic or pottery dish and covered with the cooking mixture, which serves to seal and preserve it. The word confit is also used more generally to describe a cooking method that results in the preservation of a particular ingredient, such as garlic or lemons.

STORAGE Recipe suitable for freezing.

spiced apricot & lamb tagine

PREPARATION TIME 20 MINUTES COOKING TIME 2 HOURS

60ml OLIVE OIL
1kg DICED LAMB
2 CLOVES GARLIC, CRUSHED
1 LARGE BROWN ONION (200g), CHOPPED FINELY
1/4 TEASPOON GROUND CINNAMON
1/2 TEASPOON GROUND CUMIN
1/2 TEASPOON GROUND GINGER
1/2 TEASPOON GROUND TURMERIC
750ml WATER
1 CINNAMON STICK
2 STRIPS LEMON RIND
1 1/2 TABLESPOONS HONEY
150g DRIED APRICOTS
80g BLANCHED ALMONDS, TOASTED
2 TABLESPOONS COARSELY CHOPPED FRESH CORIANDER
1 TABLESPOON SESAME SEEDS, TOASTED

1   Heat oil in large saucepan; cook lamb, in batches, stirring, until browned. Remove from pan.
2   Add garlic, onion and ground spices to pan; cook, stirring, until onion is soft. Stir in the water, cinnamon stick and lemon rind.
3   Return lamb to pan; simmer, covered, about 1 1/2 hours or until lamb is tender.
4   Add honey, apricots and nuts to lamb mixture; simmer, uncovered, 10 minutes or until apricots are tender. Discard cinnamon stick and rind; stir in chopped coriander.
5   Serve sprinkled with sesame seeds.

SERVES 4
PER SERVING 35.8g FAT; 2815KJ (672 CAL)

spicy coconut lamb

PREPARATION TIME 15 MINUTES
COOKING TIME 1 HOUR 45 MINUTES

STORAGE Recipe can be made a day ahead and refrigerated, covered. Recipe suitable for freezing; stir in nuts and coconut milk after reheating.

40g BUTTER
4 DRIED CURRY LEAVES
2 MEDIUM BROWN ONIONS (300g),
SLICED THICKLY
½ TEASPOON CHILLI POWDER
1 TEASPOON GROUND TURMERIC
1 TEASPOON GROUND CUMIN
2 TEASPOONS GROUND CORIANDER
5 CLOVES GARLIC, CRUSHED
3 TEASPOONS GRATED FRESH GINGER
1kg DICED LAMB
2 TABLESPOONS MALT VINEGAR
425g CAN TOMATOES
625ml WATER
4 CARDAMOM PODS, BRUISED
1 CINNAMON STICK
2 STRIPS LEMON RIND
4 SMALL POTATOES (480g), CHOPPED
COARSELY
4 SMALL AUBERGINES (240g),
CHOPPED COARSELY
30g GROUND ALMONDS
180ml COCONUT MILK

1   Heat butter in large saucepan; cook curry leaves, onion, chilli powder, ground spices, garlic and ginger; stirring until fragrant.

2   Add lamb; stir until browned lightly. Add vinegar, undrained crushed tomatoes, water, cardamom, cinnamon and rind; simmer, covered, 30 minutes.

3   Add potatoes; simmer, covered, about 30 minutes or until lamb is tender.

4   Add aubergines to lamb mixture; simmer, uncovered, 30 minutes. Discard leaves, whole spices and rind; stir in nuts and coconut milk.

SERVES 6
PER SERVING   21.2g FAT; 1795KJ
(429 CAL)

persian lamb and rhubarb stew

PREPARATION TIME 20 MINUTES   COOKING TIME 2 HOURS 10 MINUTES

Ordinary lamb comes from animals younger than 12months. Spring lamb comes from animals 3 to 10 months old and has a sweet and delicate flavour. The flavour of lamb is sweet and works very well with many fresh and dried fruits – either as an accompaniment or cooked with the meat as shown in this recipe.

40g BUTTER
1kg DICED LAMB
1 MEDIUM BROWN ONION (150g), SLICED THINLY
1/4 TEASPOON SAFFRON THREADS
1/2 TEASPOON GROUND CINNAMON
1/4 TEASPOON GROUND TURMERIC
250ml WATER
500ml CHICKEN STOCK
2 TABLESPOONS TOMATO PASTE
300g COARSELY CHOPPED RHUBARB
3 TABLESPOONS FINELY CHOPPED FRESH MINT

1   Melt half of the butter in large deep saucepan; cook lamb, in batches, until browned all over.
2   Melt remaining butter in same pan; cook onion, stirring, until soft. Add spices; cook, stirring, until fragrant. Add the water, stock and paste; bring to a boil. Return lamb to pan, reduce heat; simmer, covered, 1 hour 20 minutes, stirring occasionally.
3   Uncover; simmer about 20 minutes or until lamb is tender. Add rhubarb to lamb mixture; simmer, uncovered, about 10 minutes or until rhubarb has softened.
4   Stir mint into stew off the heat.
5   Serve stew with olive and parsley couscous (see page 88).

SERVES 4
PER SERVING (INCL. COUSCOUS)   FAT 38.4g; 3766KJ (901 CAL)

TIPS Make sure the rhubarb you use is a rich, strong red colour; otherwise the flavour of the finished stew will be too tart. Frozen rhubarb can be substituted for fresh.

STORAGE Recipe suitable for freezing.

pork

pork with beans & beer

3 CLOVES GARLIC, CRUSHED
1/2 TEASPOON FRESHLY GROUND
BLACK PEPPER
1.8kg PORK NECK
1 TABLESPOON OLIVE OIL
3 BACON RASHERS (215g), CHOPPED
FINELY
2 MEDIUM BROWN ONIONS (300g),
SLICED THINLY
2 TEASPOONS CARAWAY SEEDS
375ml CAN BEER
200g DRIED HARICOT BEANS
375ml CHICKEN STOCK
1/4 SMALL (300g) WHITE CABBAGE,
SHREDDED FINELY

PREPARATION TIME 20 MINUTES   COOKING TIME 2 HOURS
20 MINUTES

1   Rub combined garlic and pepper all over pork. Secure pork with
string at 2cm (¾in) intervals to make an even shape.
2   Heat oil in 5 litre large flameproof casserole dish. Cook pork,
turning, until browned all over. Remove from dish.
3   Cook bacon, onion and seeds in dish, stirring, until onion is soft
and bacon browned lightly.
4   Return pork to dish. Add beer, beans and stock; simmer, covered,
about 2 hours or until beans and pork are tender.
5   Remove pork from dish. Add shredded cabbage; cook, stirring,
until just wilted.

SERVES 8
PER SERVING   13g FAT; 1754KJ (419 CAL)

TIPS We used a dish with a base measuring 23cm (9in), so the
pork was covered with liquid during cooking. Any small white
dried bean can be used.

STORAGE Recipe can be made a day ahead and refrigerated,
covered. Recipe suitable for freezing.

pork

pork, apples & prunes

2 TABLESPOONS VEGETABLE OIL
2 SMALL LEEKS (400g), SLICED THINLY
4 FOREQUARTER PORK CHOPS
(1.75Kg)
PLAIN FLOUR
1 LITRE CHICKEN STOCK
100g LONG-GRAIN RICE
4 MEDIUM APPLES (600g), SLICED
THICKLY
170g STONED PRUNES
2 TABLESPOONS COARSELY
CHOPPED FRESH SAGE

PREPARATION TIME 25 MINUTES   COOKING TIME 1 HOUR
30 MINUTES

1   Heat one-third of the oil in 2.5 litre flameproof casserole dish;
cook leek, stirring, until soft. Remove from dish.
2   Trim fat and bone from chops; cut pork into 5cm (2in) pieces.
Toss pork in flour; shake away excess flour.
3   Heat remaining oil in dish; cook pork, stirring, until browned.
Add leek and stock to dish; cook, covered, in moderate oven
45 minutes.
4   Remove dish from oven; skim off any fat. Stir in rice, apple,
prunes and half of the sage; cook, covered, about 20 minutes or
until pork is tender.
5   Serve sprinkled with remaining sage.

SERVES 4
PER SERVING FAT 22.7g; 2978KJ (711 CAL)

STORAGE Recipe can
be made a day ahead and
refrigerated, covered. Recipe
suitable for freezing.

ham hock with sweet vegetables

40g BUTTER
2 HAM HOCKS (1.5kg)
80ml DRY RED WINE
500ml CHICKEN STOCK
2 MEDIUM POTATOES (400g),
CHOPPED COARSELY
I MEDIUM BROWN ONION
(150g), CHOPPED COARSELY
3 SMALL AUBERGINES (180g),
CHOPPED COARSELY
I SMALL SWEDE (150g),
CHOPPED COARSELY
300g BUTTERNUT SQUASH,
CHOPPED COARSELY
I MEDIUM CARROT (120g),
CHOPPED COARSELY
125ml TOMATO PUREE
I LARGE COURGETTE (150g),
CHOPPED COARSELY
150g BUTTON MUSHROOMS,
HALVED
I TABLESPOON COARSELY
CHOPPED FRESH BASIL

PREPARATION TIME 25 MINUTES   COOKING TIME 45 MINUTES

1   Heat butter in large pan; cook ham hocks until browned lightly.
2   Add wine and chicken stock. Cover; simmer about 1 hour until ham is tender.
3   Add potato, onion, aubergines, swede, butternut squash, carrot and tomato puree; simmer, uncovered 10 minutes. Add courgette, mushrooms and basil; simmer, covered, about 15 minutes or until vegetables are tender.
4   Remove ham from bones and serve with vegetables and sauce.

SERVES 6
PER SERVING   13.5g FAT; 1355KJ (324 CAL)

maple-syrup pork with pecans

PREPARATION TIME 20 MINUTES COOKING TIME 1 HOUR 50 MINUTES

1kg BONED PORK BELLY, CUT INTO FOUR PIECES
250ml PURE MAPLE SYRUP
750ml CHICKEN STOCK
1 CINNAMON STICK
2 DRIED ANCHO CHILLIES
6 WHOLE CLOVES
2 CLOVES GARLIC, CRUSHED
125ml SOY SAUCE
125ml ORANGE JUICE
1 TABLESPOON OLIVE OIL
750g SWISS CHARD, TRIMMED, SLICED THINLY
60g COARSELY CHOPPED ROASTED PECANS

1 Combine pork, maple syrup, stock, cinnamon, chillies, cloves, garlic and soy in saucepan large enough to hold pork in a single layer; bring to a boil. Reduce heat; simmer, covered, about 1½ hours or until pork is tender, turning pork every 30 minutes. Remove pork; cover to keep warm. Stir juice into braising liquid; bring to a boil. Reduce heat; simmer, uncovered, about 5 minutes or until sauce thickens slightly. Strain sauce into small bowl.
2 Meanwhile, heat oil in large saucepan; cook Swiss chard, stirring, about 5 minutes or until wilted.
3 Cut each pork piece into quarters. Divide Swiss chard among plates; top with pork, drizzle with sauce then sprinkle with nuts. Serve with steamed basmati and wild rice blend, if desired.

SERVES 4
PER SERVING 67.2g FAT; 4080KJ (976 CAL)

PECANS Many cooks think pecans are only suitable used in desserts, but they are just as good in salads, stuffings and main courses. They are also great tossed in curry spices then roasted or coated in chocolate or toffee. Studies show that pecans contain the most antioxidants of any nut and about 60 per cent of their fat content is considered to be 'good' monounsaturated fats.

TIP Ancho chillies, the most commonly used chilli in Mexico, are poblano chillies which have been dried. Having a fruity, sweet and smoky flavour, they measure about 8cm (3¼in) in length and are dark reddish brown in colour.

STORAGE Recipe is suitable for freezing.

TIPS Chipotle chillies, also known as ahumado, are jalapeño chillies that have been dried then smoked. They are about 6cm (2½in) in length, a dark brown, almost black, colour and have a deep, intense smoky flavour rather than a blast of heat. They are available from herb and spice shops as well as many gourmet delicatessens.

STORAGE Recipe suitable for freezing.

pork ribs with chilli & smoked paprika

4 CHIPOTLE CHILLIES
250ml BOILING WATER
1.5kg PORK BELLY RIBS
1 TABLESPOON OLIVE OIL
1 CHORIZO (170g), SLICED THINLY
2 MEDIUM RED ONIONS (340g), CHOPPED COARSELY
1 MEDIUM RED PEPPER (200g), CHOPPED COARSELY
1 MEDIUM GREEN PEPPER (200g), CHOPPED COARSELY
1 TEASPOON SMOKED PAPRIKA
4 CLOVES GARLIC, CRUSHED
3 X 400g CANS CRUSHED TOMATOES
2 MEDIUM TOMATOES (300g), CHOPPED FINELY
30g FINELY CHOPPED FRESH CORIANDER
2 TEASPOONS FINELY GRATED LIME RIND
1 CLOVE GARLIC, CRUSHED, EXTRA

PREPARATION TIME 20 MINUTES COOKING TIME 2 HOURS 50 MINUTES

1 Preheat oven to moderately low.
2 Soak chillies in the boiling water in small heatproof bowl for 10 minutes. Discard stalks from chillies; reserve chillies and liquid.
3 Using heavy knife, separate ribs. Heat oil in large deep flameproof baking dish; cook ribs, in batches, until browned all over.
4 Cook chorizo, onion, peppers, paprika and garlic in same dish, stirring, until onion softens. Return ribs to dish with undrained crushed tomatoes, chillies and reserved liquid. Cover; cook in moderately low oven about 1 hour.
5 Uncover; cook in moderately low oven about 1½ hours or until ribs are tender.
6 Meanwhile, combine chopped tomato, coriander, rind and extra garlic in small bowl. Cover; refrigerate until required.
7 Top ribs with coriander mixture; serve with roasted corn salsa (see page 89) and flour tortillas, if desired.

SERVES 4
PER SERVING (INCL. SALSA) 97.7g FAT; 5300KJ (1268 CAL)

sweet & sour tamarind pork

PREPARATION TIME 25 MINUTES COOKING TIME 50 MINUTES

2 TABLESPOONS PEANUT OIL
4 PORK FOREQUARTER CHOPS (1kg)
1 TABLESPOON CHINESE COOKING WINE
250ml CHICKEN STOCK
80ml TAMARIND CONCENTRATE
60ml SOY SAUCE
65g GRATED PALM SUGAR
1 MEDIUM RED PEPPER (200g), SLICED THICKLY
1 MEDIUM GREEN PEPPER (200g), SLICED THICKLY
1 MEDIUM RED ONION (170g), SLICED THICKLY
3 SPRING ONIONS, SLICED THICKLY

AROMATIC PASTE
4cm (1½in) PIECE FRESH GALANGAL (20g), CHOPPED FINELY
20cm (8in) STICK FRESH LEMON-GRASS (40g), CHOPPED FINELY
2 CLOVES GARLIC, QUARTERED
2 SHALLOTS (50g), CHOPPED COARSELY
1 TABLESPOON SAMBAL OELEK

1 Preheat oven to low.
2 Blend or process ingredients for aromatic paste until mixture becomes a thick coarse puree.
3 Heat half of the oil in large deep flameproof baking dish; cook pork, in batches, until browned both sides.
4 Heat remaining oil in same dish; cook aromatic paste, stirring, until fragrant. Return pork to dish with wine, stock, tamarind, soy, sugar, peppers and red onion; bring to a boil. Cover; cook in low oven 25 minutes, turning pork once halfway through cooking time.
5 Add spring onion; cook, covered, in slow oven about 10 minutes or until spring onion is tender. Serve with steamed rice, if desired.

SERVES 4
PER SERVING 31.8g FAT; 2462KJ (589 CAL)

pork

TIP Also known as ka, galangal is a rhizome with a hot ginger-citrusy flavour that is used similarly to ginger and garlic as a seasoning and as an ingredient. Sometimes known as Thai, Siamese or Laos ginger, it also comes in a powdered form called laos. Fresh ginger can be used instead of fresh galangal but the flavour of the dish will not be exactly the same.

TIP Ask your butcher to remove the rind and slice the pork for you.

STORAGE Recipe is suitable for freezing.

pork, chicken & black-eyed bean cassoulet

PREPARATION TIME 20 MINUTES (PLUS STANDING TIME)
COOKING TIME 2 HOURS 45 MINUTES

200g BLACK-EYED BEANS
1 TABLESPOON OLIVE OIL
500g BONED PORK BELLY, RIND REMOVED, SLICED THINLY
8 CHICKEN DRUMSTICKS (640g)
4 THIN PORK SAUSAGES (320g)
1 TRIMMED CELERY STALK (100g), SLICED THINLY
1 MEDIUM BROWN ONION (150g), CHOPPED COARSELY
1 SMALL LEEK (200g), SLICED THINLY
1 TEASPOON FRESH THYME LEAVES
125ml DRY WHITE WINE
400g CAN CHOPPED TOMATOES
500ml CHICKEN STOCK
210g STALE BREADCRUMBS
30g FINELY CHOPPED FRESH FLAT-LEAF PARSLEY
50g BUTTER, MELTED

1 Place beans in medium bowl, cover with cold water; stand 3 hours or overnight, drain. Rinse under cold water; drain.
2 Preheat oven to moderate.
3 Heat oil in large flameproof casserole dish; cook pork, chicken and sausages, in batches, until browned all over.
4 Cook celery, onion, leek and thyme in same dish, stirring, until onion softens. Add wine; cook, stirring, 5 minutes. Return pork, chicken and sausages to dish with undrained tomatoes, stock and beans; cook, covered in moderate oven 40 minutes.
5 Uncover; sprinkle with combined breadcrumbs, parsley and butter. Cook, uncovered, in moderate oven about 40 minutes or until meat is tender and top is lightly browned. Serve with a curly endive salad dressed with white wine vinaigrette, if desired.

SERVES 4
PER SERVING 65.2g FAT; 4314KJ (1032 CAL)

BLACK-EYED BEANS
Also called black-eyed peas or cow peas, the small, kidney-shaped, white bean with a single black spot used here has a fairly thin skin so cooks rather faster than other legumes. A good source of protein and complex carbohydrates, beans keep their nutritional value even through lengthy storage.

asian chicken pot au feu

PREPARATION TIME 30 MINUTES COOKING TIME 1 HOUR 30 MINUTES

4 LITRES WATER
1.5kg CHICKEN
2 CLOVES GARLIC, BRUISED
2 LARGE CARROTS (360g), HALVED, QUARTERED LENGTHWAYS
10cm (4in) STICK FRESH LEMONGRASS (20g), BRUISED
2 FRESH KAFFIR LIME LEAVES
2cm (¾in) PIECE GALANGAL (10g), SLICED THINLY
2 FRESH LONG RED CHILLIES, HALVED LENGTHWAYS
1 TEASPOON SICHUAN PEPPERCORNS
½ TEASPOON FIVE-SPICE POWDER
60ml MIRIN
125ml SOY SAUCE
80ml KECAP MANIS
350g BROCCOLINI, CHOPPED COARSELY

1 Bring the water to a boil in large deep saucepan. Add chicken, garlic, carrot, lemongrass, lime leaves, galangal, chilli, peppercorns, five-spice, mirin, sauce and kecap manis; return to a boil. Reduce heat; simmer, uncovered, 1 hour; skimming fat from surface occasionally. (Chicken suitable for freezing at this stage.)
2 Remove chicken; strain broth through muslin-lined sieve into large bowl. Reserve carrot; discard remaining solids. Cover chicken and carrot to keep warm. Return all but 500ml of the broth to same saucepan; bring to a boil. Cook broccolini in large saucepan of boiling broth, uncovered, until just tender; drain over large bowl. Reserve broth for another use.
3 Meanwhile, place the 500ml of broth in small saucepan; bring to a boil. Boil rapidly, uncovered, until reduced to 250ml.
4 Serve chicken with carrot, broccolini, reduced broth and, if desired, steamed jasmine rice.

SERVES 4
PER SERVING 28.6g FAT; 2082KJ (498 CAL)

KAFFIR LIME LEAVES
look like two glossy dark-green leaves joined end to end, forming a rounded hourglass shape. They are used, fresh or dried, as a flavouring, like bay leaves or curry leaves, through-out Asia, especially in Thai cooking. Sold fresh, dried or frozen, the dried leaves are less potent so double the number called for in a recipe if you substitute them for fresh leaves.

chicken

classic coq au vin

1.5kg CHICKEN PIECES
PLAIN FLOUR
40g BUTTER
2 CLOVES GARLIC, CRUSHED
3 BACON RASHERS (215g), CHOPPED FINELY
10 SPRING ONIONS (250g), TRIMMED
200g CHESTNUT MUSHROOMS, HALVED
2 TABLESPOONS BRANDY
250ml DRY RED WINE
250ml CHICKEN STOCK
1 SPRIG FRESH PARSLEY
2 TEASPOONS FINELY CHOPPED FRESH THYME
1 BAY LEAF
2 TABLESPOONS TOMATO PASTE

PREPARATION TIME 20 MINUTES COOKING TIME 1 HOUR

1 Toss chicken in flour; shake away excess flour. Heat butter in large saucepan; cook chicken until browned all over. Drain on kitchen paper.
2 Drain all but 1 tablespoon of the liquid from pan; cook garlic, bacon, onion and mushrooms, stirring, until onion is browned lightly.
3 Return chicken to pan. Add brandy, wine, stock, herbs, bay leaf and paste; simmer, covered, 30 minutes or until chicken is tender.
4 Remove chicken from pan; simmer sauce until thickened slightly. Discard bay leaf before serving.
5 Serve chicken with sauce.

SERVES 4
PER SERVING 48.3g FAT; 3170KJ (757 CAL)

curried lemon chicken

12 CHICKEN THIGHS (2kg)
PLAIN FLOUR
2 TABLESPOONS VEGETABLE OIL
1 MEDIUM LEEK (350g), CHOPPED
COARSELY
2 TRIMMED STICKS CELERY (150g),
SLICED THINLY
2 CLOVES GARLIC, CRUSHED
2 TEASPOONS MILD CURRY POWDER
1 TABLESPOON LEMON JUICE
1 LARGE GREEN PEPPER (350g),
CHOPPED FINELY
250g BUTTON MUSHROOMS
750ml CHICKEN STOCK

PREPARATION TIME 20 MINUTES **COOKING TIME** 1 HOUR
20 MINUTES

1 Remove skin from chicken. Toss chicken in flour; shake away
excess flour.
2 Heat oil in 3 litre flameproof casserole dish; cook chicken, in
batches, until browned. Drain on absorbent paper.
3 Add leek, celery, garlic and curry powder to dish; cook, stirring,
until leek is soft. Add juice, capsicum and mushrooms; cook, stirring,
2 minutes or until liquid evaporates.
4 Add chicken and stock; mix gently.
5 Cook, covered, in moderate oven about 1 hour or until chicken
is tender.

SERVES 6
PER SERVING 24g FAT; 1862KJ (445 CAL)

STORAGE Recipe can
be made a day ahead and
refrigerated, covered. Recipe
suitable for freezing.

chicken cacciatore

4 CHICKEN LEG JOINTS (1.4kg)
PLAIN FLOUR
1 TABLESPOON OLIVE OIL
2 CLOVES GARLIC, CRUSHED
4 SLICES PANCETTA (60g), CHOPPED
COARSELY
1 LARGE BROWN ONION (200g),
CHOPPED FINELY
1 MEDIUM (200g) YELLOW PEPPER,
CHOPPED COARSELY
3 MEDIUM TOMATOES (450g), PEELED,
CHOPPED COARSELY
125ml DRY WHITE WINE
125ml TOMATO PUREE
2 TEASPOONS FINELY CHOPPED
FRESH SAGE
1 TEASPOON FINELY CHOPPED
FRESH ROSEMARY
1 BAY LEAF

PREPARATION TIME 20 MINUTES   COOKING TIME 55 MINUTES

1   Cut chicken through joint into two pieces. Toss chicken in flour;
shake away excess flour.
2   Heat oil in large saucepan; cook chicken, in batches, until browned
all over. Drain on kitchen paper.
3   Drain all but 1 tablespoon of the juices from pan; cook garlic,
pancetta, onion and pepper, stirring, until onion is soft. Add tomato,
wine and puree; simmer, uncovered, 2 minutes.
4   Return chicken to pan. Add herbs and bay leaf; simmer, covered,
about 30 minutes or until chicken is tender. Discard bay leaf before
serving.

SERVES 4
PER SERVING   39.5g FAT; 2636KJ (630 CAL)

STORAGE   Recipe can
be made a day ahead and
refrigerated, covered. Recipe
suitable for freezing.

1kg CHICKEN THIGH FILLETS
2 TEASPOONS GROUND ALLSPICE
1 TEASPOON GROUND CINNAMON
PINCH GROUND NUTMEG
1 TABLESPOON FINELY CHOPPED
FRESH THYME
60ml OLIVE OIL
2 MEDIUM BROWN ONIONS (300g),
SLICED THINLY
2 CLOVES GARLIC, CRUSHED
1 TABLESPOON GRATED FRESH
GINGER
1 TEASPOON SAMBAL OELEK
5 MEDIUM TOMATOES (650g), PEELED,
DESEEDED, CHOPPED FINELY
2 TABLESPOONS BROWN SUGAR
2 TEASPOONS GRATED ORANGE
RIND
2 TABLESPOONS SOY SAUCE
1 MEDIUM SWEET POTATO (400g),
CHOPPED COARSELY
2 FRESH CORN COBS, SLICED
THICKLY
125g BABY SPINACH LEAVES

spicy caribbean-style chicken stew

PREPARATION TIME 45 MINUTES COOKING TIME 50 MINUTES

1 Cut chicken into 2cm (¾in) strips. Toss chicken in combined spices and thyme.
2 Heat half of the oil in large saucepan; cook chicken, in batches, stirring, until browned. Drain on kitchen paper.
3 Heat remaining oil in pan. Cook onion, garlic, ginger and sambal oelek, stirring, until onion is soft.
4 Add tomato, sugar, rind, sauce, sweet potato, corn and chicken; cook, covered, about 15 minutes or until chicken and vegetables are tender. Remove cover; simmer 5 minutes.
5 Remove from heat. Add spinach; stir until spinach is wilted.

SERVES 6
PER SERVING 22.3g FAT; 1998KJ (477 CAL)

chicken, date and honey tagine

PREPARATION TIME 20 MINUTES (PLUS REFRIGERATING AND STANDING TIME) COOKING TIME 50 MINUTES

1 TEASPOON SALT
1 TEASPOON CRACKED BLACK PEPPER
1/2 TEASPOON GROUND SAFFRON
2 TEASPOONS GROUND CUMIN
8 CHICKEN THIGH CUTLETS (1.2kg)
30g BUTTER
1 TABLESPOON OLIVE OIL
1 LARGE BROWN ONION (200g), CHOPPED FINELY
1 CINNAMON STICK
375ml WATER
6 STONELESS FRESH DATES (150g)
2 TEASPOONS HONEY
40g BLANCHED ALMONDS, TOASTED

DATES The fruits of the date palm tree, thought to have originated in North Africa, which have a thick, sticky texture and sweet mild flavour. Sometimes dates are sold already stoned and chopped. They can be eaten fresh or dried on their own, or cooked to release their flavour.

1 Rub combined salt, pepper, saffron and cumin onto chicken. Cover; refrigerate 2 hours or overnight.
2 Heat butter and oil in large saucepan; cook chicken until browned. Remove from pan; drain all but 1 tablespoon of the liquid from pan. Add onion and cinnamon to pan; cook, stirring, until onion is soft.
3 Return chicken to pan. Add the water; simmer, covered, about 30 minutes or until chicken is tender. Add dates and honey; simmer, uncovered, 10 minutes or until thickened slightly.
4 Serve tagine with saffron couscous (see page 88), sprinkled with nuts.

SERVES 4
PER SERVING 40.8g FAT; 3708KJ (886 CAL) (INCLUDING COUSCOUS)

african-style peanut, okra & tomato gumbo

PREPARATION TIME 30 MINUTES
COOKING TIME 50 MINUTES

300g OKRA
2 TABLESPOONS PEANUT OIL
800g CHICKEN THIGH FILLETS, CHOPPED COARSELY
2 LARGE BROWN ONIONS (400g), SLICED THICKLY
3 CLOVES GARLIC, CRUSHED
I TEASPOON SAMBAL OELEK
5 MEDIUM TOMATOES (650g), PEELED, DESEEDED, CHOPPED FINELY
70g TOMATO PASTE
85g CRUNCHY PEANUT BUTTER
I LARGE POTATO (300g), CHOPPED COARSELY
500ml WATER

I Trim stems from okra. Heat half of the oil in large saucepan; cook chicken, in batches, stirring, until browned. Drain on absorbent paper.
2 Heat remaining oil in pan; cook onion, garlic and sambal oelek, stirring, until onion is soft.
3 Return chicken to pan. Add remaining ingredients; simmer, covered, about 30 minutes or until potato is tender.

SERVES 4
PER SERVING 34.5g FAT; 2517KJ (601 CAL)

green chicken curry with vegetables

PREPARATION TIME 35 MINUTES
COOKING TIME 50 MINUTES

2 TABLESPOONS PEANUT OIL
1 LARGE BROWN ONION (200g),
SLICED THICKLY
1 MEDIUM GREEN PEPPER (200g),
CHOPPED COARSELY
250ml CHICKEN STOCK
280ml CAN COCONUT MILK
1 DRIED LIME LEAF
360g BABY PAK CHOY, CHOPPED COARSELY
2 TEASPOONS CORNFLOUR
2 TEASPOONS WATER
3 TABLESPOONS FINELY SHREDDED BASIL

CURRY PASTE
1 SMALL FRESH GREEN CHILLI
2 TABLESPOONS FINELY CHOPPED
FRESH LEMONGRASS
1 TABLESPOON GRATED FRESH GINGER
2 CLOVES GARLIC, CRUSHED
1 TABLESPOON FISH SAUCE
1 TABLESPOON PALM SUGAR
1 TEASPOON GROUND CORIANDER
1/2 TEASPOON GROUND CUMIN
1/2 TEASPOON GROUND GINGER

1   Cut each fillet into three pieces. Heat half of the oil in large saucepan; cook chicken, in batches, until browned. Remove from pan.
2   Heat remaining oil in pan; cook onion, pepper and curry paste, stirring, until onion is soft.
3   Return chicken to pan. Add stock, coconut milk and lime leaf; simmer, uncovered, about 20 minutes or until chicken is tender, stirring occasionally.
4   Add pak choy and blended cornflour and water; cook, stirring, until mixture boils and thickens slightly. Stir in basil. Discard lime leaf before serving.

CURRY PASTE   Blend or process ingredients until combined.

SERVES 4
PER SERVING   38.1g FAT; 2652KJ (633 CAL)

STORAGE   Recipe best
made just before serving.

creamy chicken korma

PREPARATION TIME 25 MINUTES (PLUS REFRIGERATION TIME)
COOKING TIME 1 HOUR

35g UNSALTED CASHEWS
1 TEASPOON SESAME SEEDS
500g PLAIN YOGURT
3 CLOVES GARLIC, CRUSHED
2cm (¾in) PIECE FRESH GINGER (10g), GRATED
1 TEASPOON DRIED CHILLI FLAKES
½ TEASPOON GROUND TURMERIC
1kg CHICKEN THIGH FILLETS, DICED INTO 3cm (1in) PIECES
2 TABLESPOONS VEGETABLE OIL
2 MEDIUM BROWN ONIONS (300g), SLICED THINLY
2 CARDAMOM PODS
2 WHOLE CLOVES
½ TEASPOON BLACK CUMIN SEEDS
½ CINNAMON STICK
2 TABLESPOONS LEMON JUICE
15g FLAKED COCONUT
50g UNSALTED CASHEWS, EXTRA
2 TEASPOONS KALONJI SEEDS
3 TABLESPOONS LOOSELY PACKED FRESH CORIANDER LEAVES

1   Process nuts and sesame seeds until ground finely. Combine nut mixture with yogurt, garlic, ginger, chilli and turmeric in large bowl; add chicken, toss to coat in marinade. Cover; refrigerate 3 hours or overnight.
2   Heat oil in large saucepan; cook onion, stirring, until soft. Add chicken mixture. Reduce heat; simmer, uncovered, 40 minutes, stirring occasionally.
3   Using mortar and pestle, crush cardamom, cloves and cumin seeds.
4   Add spice mixture, cinnamon and juice to chicken mixture; cook, uncovered, about 10 minutes or until chicken is cooked through.
5   Meanwhile, cook coconut and extra nuts in small frying pan, stirring, until browned lightly. Remove from heat; stir in kalonji seeds.
5   Discard cinnamon from curry; serve curry, sprinkled with coconut mixture and coriander, accompanied by steamed basmati rice, if desired.

SERVES 4
PER SERVING 45.7g FAT; 2918KJ (698 CAL)

KALONJI Also known as nigella, kalonji are angular purple-black seeds which are a creamy colour inside and possess a sharp, nutty taste. They are the seeds sprinkled over the top of freshly made pide, Turkish bread, that give it a special sharp, peppery flavour. Kalonji are found in spice shops and Middle-Eastern and Asian food stores.them for fresh leaves.

STORAGE Seasoning can be made a day ahead; casserole can be made 3 hours ahead and refrigerated, covered.

8 CHICKEN DRUMSTICKS (1.2kg)
PLAIN FLOUR
2 TEASPOONS VEGETABLE OIL
250ml BEER
125ml CHICKEN STOCK
1 TABLESPOON WORCESTERSHIRE
SAUCE
2 TEASPOONS CORNFLOUR
2 TEASPOONS WATER

HERB SEASONING
2 BACON RASHERS (140g),
CHOPPED FINELY
45g STALE BREADCRUMBS
40g BUTTER, MELTED
1 TABLESPOON FINELY CHOPPED
FRESH OREGANO
1 TABLESPOON FINELY CHOPPED
FRESH CHIVES
2 TEASPOONS FINELY CHOPPED
FRESH THYME
1 TEASPOON SEASONED PEPPER

irish herb chicken

PREPARATION TIME 25 MINUTES COOKING TIME 40 MINUTES

1 Push herb seasoning under skin of drumsticks; toss in flour.
Shake away excess flour.
2 Heat oil in large saucepan; cook chicken, in batches, until
browned.
3 Return chicken to pan. Add beer, stock and sauce; simmer,
covered, about 20 minutes or until chicken is tender, stirring
occasionally. Add blended cornflour and water; cook, stirring, until
sauce boils and thickens.
4 Serve with pasta, if desired.

HERB SEASONING Heat large saucepan; cook bacon, stirring, until
browned. Remove from heat; stir in remaining ingredients.

SERVES 4
PER SERVING 31.5g FAT; 2169KJ (518 CAL)

chicken

chicken cassoulet

200g DRIED HARICOT BEANS
500g SPICY ITALIAN SAUSAGES
250g PORK SAUSAGES
4 CHICKEN THIGHS (900g)
4 SINGLE CHICKEN BREASTS ON THE BONE (1kg)
1 TABLESPOON VEGETABLE OIL
3 BACON RASHERS (215g), SLICED THINLY
2 CLOVES GARLIC, CRUSHED
3 CLOVES
12 BLACK PEPPERCORNS
1 TRIMMED STICK CELERY (75g), CUT INTO 5cm (2in) LENGTHS
4 MEDIUM CARROTS (480g), SLICED THINLY
5 BABY ONIONS (125g), HALVED
125ml DRY WHITE WINE
750ml WATER
2 TABLESPOONS TOMATO PASTE

PREPARATION TIME 25 MINUTES (PLUS STANDING TIME)
COOKING TIME 2 HOURS 30 MINUTES

1 Place beans in large bowl; cover well with cold water. Cover; stand overnight.
2 Drain beans. Add sausages to large saucepan of boiling water. Boil, uncovered, 2 minutes; drain.
3 Remove skin from chicken; cut breasts in half.
4 Heat oil in 5 litre flameproof casserole dish; cook chicken and sausages, in batches, until browned. Drain on absorbent paper; slice sausages thickly.
5 Add bacon; cook, stirring, until crisp. Drain on kitchen paper.
6 Return chicken to dish with beans, garlic, cloves, peppercorns, celery, carrot, onion, wine, the water and paste. Cook, covered, in moderate oven 1½ hours.
7 Add sausages; cover. Cook about 30 minutes or until sausages are cooked. Serve sprinkled with bacon.

SERVES 8
PER SERVING 42.1g FAT; 2960KJ (707 CAL)

japanese seafood hotpot

PREPARATION TIME 20 MINUTES (PLUS REFRIGERATION TIME)
COOKING TIME 20 MINUTES

DASHI is the basic stock used in nearly every Japanese dish, from a spoonful or two in dipping sauces to far greater amounts in the broths of one-pan dishes such as shabu-shabu, sukiyaki or casserole-like hotpots such as the one we've made here. Available in concentrated liquid as well as granule or powdered form, the amount of dashi used can be adjusted to suit your personal taste.

12 MEDIUM BLACK MUSSELS (300g)
12 UNCOOKED MEDIUM KING PRAWNS (540g)
2 TEASPOONS COOKING SAKE
1 TABLESPOON JAPANESE SOY SAUCE
2 TEASPOONS MIRIN
12 SCALLOPS WITHOUT ROE (300g)
400g FIRM WHITE FISH FILLETS, DICED INTO 4cm (1½in) PIECES
1 TABLESPOON VEGETABLE OIL
2 CLOVES GARLIC, CRUSHED
5cm (2in) PIECE FRESH GINGER (25g), CHOPPED FINELY
750ml FISH STOCK
250ml WATER
60ml COOKING SAKE, EXTRA
60ml JAPANESE SOY SAUCE, EXTRA
1 TEASPOON POWDERED DASHI
1 SMALL SWEET POTATO (250g), HALVED LENGTHWAYS, SLICED THINLY
250g SPINACH, CHOPPED COARSELY
2 SPRING ONIONS, CHOPPED COARSELY
270g DRIED UDON NOODLES

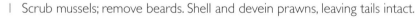

1 Scrub mussels; remove beards. Shell and devein prawns, leaving tails intact.
2 Combine sake, soy and mirin in large bowl; add mussels, prawns, scallops and fish, toss seafood to coat in mixture.
3 Heat oil in large saucepan; cook garlic and ginger, stirring, until fragrant. Add stock, the water, extra sake, extra soy and dashi; bring to a boil. Add sweet potato; cook, uncovered, 2 minutes. Add undrained seafood; cook, covered, about 5 minutes or until mussels open (discard any that do not). Add spinach and onion; cook, uncovered, until spinach just wilts.
4 Meanwhile, cook udon in large saucepan of boiling water, uncovered, until just tender; drain.
5 Divide udon among bowls; top with seafood mixture.

SERVES 4
PER SERVING 7.8g FAT; 2307KJ (552 CAL)

fish korma curry

30g GHEE
2 MEDIUM BROWN ONIONS (300g),
CHOPPED FINELY
500g SWEET POTATO, CHOPPED
COARSELY
80ml KORMA CURRY PASTE
250ml CREAM
250ml WATER
1.2kg FIRM WHITE FISH FILLETS,
CHOPPED COARSELY
1 TABLESPOON FINELY CHOPPED
FRESH CORIANDER
250g GREEN BEANS, HALVED
250g CHERRY TOMATOES

PREPARATION TIME 15 MINUTES COOKING TIME 50 MINUTES

1 Heat ghee in large saucepan; cook onion, stirring, until just tender.
Add sweet potato and paste; cook, stirring, 3 minutes.
2 Add cream and the water; simmer, covered, 30 minutes.
3 Add fish, coriander, beans and tomatoes. Stir gently; simmer,
covered, about 10 minutes or until fish is tender.

SERVES 6
PER SERVING 32.6g FAT; 3249KJ (776 CAL)

STORAGE Recipe best
made just before serving.

fish cutlets & tomato tagine

PREPARATION TIME 20 MINUTES COOKING TIME 40 MINUTES

2 TABLESPOONS OLIVE OIL

2 LARGE BROWN ONIONS (400g), CHOPPED COARSELY

6 CLOVES GARLIC, CHOPPED FINELY

1 FRESH SMALL RED THAI CHILLI, CHOPPED FINELY

4 ANCHOVY FILLETS, DRAINED, CHOPPED FINELY

40g COARSELY CHOPPED FRESH FLAT-LEAF PARSLEY

60g COARSELY CHOPPED FRESH CORIANDER

40g COARSELY CHOPPED FRESH MINT

200g MUSHROOMS, QUARTERED

2 TRIMMED CELERY STALKS (200g), SLICED THICKLY

2 TEASPOONS GROUND CUMIN

2 X 425g CANS DICED TOMATOES

4 WHITE FISH CUTLETS (1kg)

1 MEDIUM LEMON (140g), CUT INTO WEDGES

2 TABLESPOONS FRESH FLAT-LEAF PARSLEY LEAVES

1 Preheat oven to moderately hot.

2 Heat oil in large deep flameproof baking dish; cook onion, garlic and chilli, stirring, until onion softens. Add anchovy, chopped herbs, mushrooms, celery and cumin; cook, stirring, 5 minutes.

3 Add undrained tomatoes; bring to a boil. Add fish, submerging it in the tomato mixture; return to a boil. Cook, uncovered, in moderately hot oven about 20 minutes or until liquid has almost evaporated and fish is cooked as desired.

4 Divide fish and lemon wedge among serving plates; sprinkle with parsley. Serve with tomato and herb salad (see page 90) and, if desired, steamed long-grain white rice.

SERVES 4
PER SERVING (INCL. SALAD) 20.9g FAT; 2161KJ (517 CAL)

seafood stew with chermoulla

PREPARATION TIME 30 MINUTES   COOKING TIME 30 MINUTES

500g BLACK MUSSELS
800g UNCOOKED MEDIUM KING PRAWNS
300g FIRM WHITE FISH FILLET, SKINNED
1 SQUID HOOD (150g)
1 TABLESPOON OLIVE OIL
1 LARGE BROWN ONION (200g), CHOPPED FINELY
3 CLOVES GARLIC, CRUSHED
1 MEDIUM RED PEPPER (200g), CHOPPED FINELY
125ml DRY WHITE WINE
250ml FISH STOCK
400g CAN CHOPPED TOMATOES

CHERMOULLA
30g FINELY CHOPPED FRESH CORIANDER
30g FINELY CHOPPED FRESH FLAT-LEAF PARSLEY
1 CLOVE GARLIC, CRUSHED
2 TABLESPOONS WHITE WINE VINEGAR
2 TABLESPOONS LEMON JUICE
1/2 TEASPOON GROUND CUMIN
2 TABLESPOONS OLIVE OIL

CHERMOULLA is
a Moroccan blend of
fresh herbs, spices and
condiments traditionally
used for preserving or
seasoning meat and fish.
We used our chermoulla
blend here as a quick
flavouring for the stew,
but you can also use it
as a sauce or marinade.
You can keep freshly
made chermoulla in the
refrigerator, covered
with a thin layer of olive
oil to preserve it, for up
to a month.

1   Scrub mussels; remove beards. Shell and devein prawns, leaving tails intact.
Dice fish into 3cm (1in) pieces. Cut squid down centre to open out; score
inside in diagonal pattern then cut into thick strips.
2   Heat oil in large saucepan; cook onion, garlic and pepper, stirring, until
onion softens. Stir in wine; cook, uncovered, until wine is almost evaporated.
Add stock and undrained tomatoes; bring to a boil. Add seafood, reduce heat;
simmer, covered, about 5 minutes or until squid is tender and mussels open
(discard any that do not).
3   Meanwhile, combine ingredients for chermoulla in small bowl.
4   Stir half of the chermoulla into stew. Divide stew among bowls; divide
remaining chermoulla over the top of each bowl. Serve with a warmed
baguette, if desired.

SERVES 4
PER SERVING 17.5g FAT; 1714KJ (410 CAL)

lemongrass & coconut fish stew

PREPARATION TIME 20 MINUTES
(PLUS STANDING TIME)
COOKING TIME 30 MINUTES

250g DRIED EGG NOODLES
8 DRIED SHIITAKE MUSHROOMS
1 TABLESPOON VEGETABLE OIL
2 TEASPOONS GRATED FRESH GINGER
2 TABLESPOONS FINELY CHOPPED FRESH
LEMONGRASS
$1/2$ TEASPOON FIVE SPICE POWDER
1 TEASPOON GROUND TURMERIC
1 TEASPOON SAMBAL OELEK
400ml CAN COCONUT CREAM
60ml CHICKEN STOCK
1kg BONELESS WHITE FISH FILLETS,
CHOPPED COARSELY
400g BABY BOK CHOY, QUARTERED
4 SPRING ONIONS, CHOPPED FINELY

1   Add noodles to large saucepan of
boiling water. Boil, uncovered, until just
tender; drain.
2   Place mushrooms in large heatproof
bowl; cover with boiling water. Stand
20 minutes; drain mushrooms. Discard
stems; slice caps.
3   Heat oil in large saucepan; cook
ginger, lemongrass, spices, sambal oelek
and mushrooms, stirring, until fragrant.
Add coconut cream and stock; bring
to a boil. Add fish; reduce heat. Cook
covered, about 10 minutes or until fish
is just tender.
4   Stir in bok choy, onion and noodles;
reheat gently.

SERVES 6
PER SERVING 23g FAT; 2143KJ (512 CAL)

STORAGE Recipe best made just
before serving.

STORAGE Recipe best made just before serving.

seafood casserole

PREPARATION TIME 30 MINUTES
COOKING TIME 45 MINUTES

1kg SMALL MUSSELS
1kg UNCOOKED PRAWNS
500g CALAMARI HOODS
500g UNCOOKED LOBSTER TAIL
1 TABLESPOON OLIVE OIL
1 MEDIUM LEEK (350g), SLICED THINLY
4 CLOVES GARLIC, CRUSHED
425g CAN TOMATOES
180ml DRY WHITE WINE
60ml SWEET SHERRY
500ml FISH STOCK
PINCH SAFFRON THREADS
2 MEDIUM CARROTS (240g), CHOPPED FINELY
4 TABLESPOONS FINELY CHOPPED FRESH PARSLEY
1 TABLESPOON FINELY CHOPPED FRESH THYME
350g SCALLOPS

1 Scrub mussels; remove beards. Shell and devein prawns, leaving tails intact; cut calamari open. Score inside surface; cut into 6cm (2½in) pieces. Shell lobster tail; cut lobster meat into 5cm (2in) pieces.
2 Heat oil in large saucepan; cook leek and garlic, stirring, until leek is soft.
3 Add undrained crushed tomatoes, wine, sherry, stock, saffron, carrot and herbs; simmer, covered, 30 minutes.
4 Add mussels; simmer, covered, 2 minutes. Add prawns, calamari and lobster pieces; simmer, covered, about 2 minutes. Add the scallops; simmer, uncovered, about 2 minutes or until seafood is just cooked. Discard any unopened mussels.

SERVES 6
PER SERVING 6.7g FAT; 1523KJ (364 CAL)

vegetarian

chickpea vegetable braise

PREPARATION TIME 20 MINUTES (PLUS STANDING TIME)
COOKING TIME 1 HOUR 25 MINUTES

200g DRIED CHICKPEAS
2 TABLESPOONS OLIVE OIL
2 SMALL LEEKS (400g), CHOPPED
COARSELY
2 MEDIUM CARROTS (240g), CUT
INTO BATONS
2 CLOVES GARLIC, CRUSHED
1 TABLESPOON FINELY CHOPPED
FRESH ROSEMARY
2 TABLESPOONS WHITE WINE
VINEGAR
500ml VEGETABLE STOCK
100g BABY SPINACH LEAVES
60ml LEMON JUICE
2 TABLESPOONS OLIVE OIL, EXTRA
2 CLOVES GARLIC, CRUSHED, EXTRA

1 Place chickpeas in medium bowl, cover with cold water; stand overnight, drain. Rinse under cold water; drain. Place chickpeas in medium saucepan of boiling water. Return to a boil, reduce heat. Simmer chickpeas, uncovered, about 40 minutes or until they are tender. Drain.

2 Meanwhile, preheat oven to moderately low.

3 Heat oil in large deep flameproof baking dish; cook leek and carrot, stirring, until just tender. Add garlic, rosemary and chickpeas; cook, stirring, until fragrant. Add vinegar and stock; bring to a boil. Cover; cook in moderately low oven 30 minutes.

4 Remove dish from oven; stir in spinach, juice, extra oil and extra garlic.

5 Serve chickpea vegetable braise with cumin couscous (see page 88) and tomato and red onion salad (see page 90).

SERVES 4
PER SERVING (INCL. COUSCOUS AND SALAD) 31.6g FAT;
2717KJ (650 CAL)

pepper casserole with courgettes & beans

100g DRIED BORLOTTI BEANS
4 MEDIUM RED PEPPERS (800g)
4 MEDIUM COURGETTES (480g),
CHOPPED FINELY
4 BABY ONIONS (100g), QUARTERED
200g GREEN BEANS, HALVED
310g CAN CHICKPEAS, RINSED,
DRAINED
2 TABLESPOONS OLIVE OIL
20g PARMESAN CHEESE FLAKES

TOMATO SAUCE
2 X 425g CANS TOMATOES
1 TABLESPOON BALSAMIC VINEGAR
½ TEASPOON BROWN SUGAR
3 TABLESPOONS FINELY SHREDDED
FRESH BASIL

PREPARATION TIME 35 MINUTES (PLUS STANDING TIME)
COOKING TIME 1 HOUR 45 MINUTES

1 Place borlotti beans in large bowl; cover with water. Cover; stand overnight. Drain borlotti beans. Add to large saucepan of boiling water; reduce heat. Simmer, uncovered, about 20 minutes or until tender; drain.
2 Halve peppers lengthways; remove seeds and membranes. Place peppers, cut side up, in 3 litre shallow ovenproof dish.
3 Combine borlotti beans, courgettes, onion, green beans, chickpeas and oil in large bowl. Mix well; spoon into peppers. Pour over tomato sauce; cook, covered, in moderate oven 1 hour. Remove cover; cook about 15 minutes or until pepper is tender. Serve topped with parmesan cheese flakes.

TOMATO SAUCE Combine undrained crushed tomatoes, vinegar and sugar in large saucepan; simmer, uncovered, about 5 minutes or until sauce is thickened slightly. Stir in basil.

SERVES 4
PER SERVING 13.2g FAT; 1274KJ (304 CAL)

STORAGE Pepper and sauce can be prepared a day ahead and refrigerated, covered separately.

spicy okra, corn & pepper gumbo

PREPARATION TIME 30 MINUTES   COOKING TIME 1 HOUR

800g OKRA
1½ TABLESPOONS OLIVE OIL
2 MEDIUM BROWN ONIONS (300g),
CHOPPED COARSELY
4 CLOVES GARLIC, CRUSHED
1½ TEASPOONS CAJUN SEASONING
1 TEASPOON GROUND CUMIN
¼ TEASPOON CAYENNE PEPPER
3 TRIMMED STICKS CELERY (225g),
CHOPPED COARSELY
2 LARGE GREEN PEPPERS (700g),
CHOPPED COARSELY
2 LARGE RED PEPPERS (700g),
CHOPPED COARSELY
2 FRESH TRIMMED CORN COBS,
(500g) CHOPPED COARSELY
10 BABY CARROTS, CHOPPED
COARSELY
500ml VEGETABLE STOCK
2 X 425g CANS TOMATOES
2 TABLESPOONS WORCESTERSHIRE
SAUCE
100g BASMATI RICE
3 TABLESPOONS FINELY CHOPPED
FRESH PARSLEY

1   Trim stems from okra; discard stems.
2   Heat oil in large heavy-based saucepan; cook onion, garlic and spices, stirring, until onion is soft. Add celery, peppers, corn, carrot, stock, undrained crushed tomatoes and sauce; simmer, covered, 30 minutes.
3   Add rice and okra; simmer, covered, about 25 minutes or until rice is tender.
4   Serve sprinkled with parsley.

SERVES 6
PER SERVING   7.1g FAT; 1323KJ (316 CAL)

romano peppers with potato & green olive stuffing

PREPARATION TIME 50 MINUTES COOKING TIME 1 HOUR 10 MINUTES

40g BUTTER
2 TABLESPOONS OLIVE OIL
3 CLOVES GARLIC, CRUSHED
2 TEASPOONS GROUND CUMIN
2 TEASPOONS DRIED OREGANO
600g POTATOES, DICED INTO 1cm (½in) PIECES
3 LARGE TOMATOES (660g), DICED INTO 1cm (½in) PIECES
120g PITTED GREEN OLIVES, CHOPPED COARSELY
240g COARSELY GRATED CHEDDAR CHEESE
8 RED OR YELLOW ROMAMO PEPPERS (1.3kg)

TOMATO SAUCE

1 TABLESPOON OLIVE OIL
1 CLOVE GARLIC, CRUSHED
1 MEDIUM RED ONION (170g), CHOPPED COARSELY
1 TABLESPOON GROUND CUMIN
2 TEASPOONS DRIED OREGANO
2 X 425g CANS DICED TOMATOES
125ml WATER

1 Preheat oven to moderate.
2 Heat butter and oil in large frying pan; cook garlic, cumin, oregano and potato, stirring occasionally, about 10 minutes or until potato browns lightly. Add tomato and olives; cook, stirring, about 10 minutes or until liquid has evaporated. Transfer to large bowl; stir in cheese.
3 Meanwhile, using sharp knife, make a small horizontal cut in a pepper 1cm (½in) below stem, then make lengthways slit in pepper, starting from horizontal cut and ending 1cm (½in) from tip, taking care not to cut all the way through pepper; discard membrane and seeds. Repeat process with remaining peppers. Carefully divide filling among peppers, securing each closed with a toothpick.
4 Make tomato sauce. Place peppers on tomato sauce in dish, cover; cook in moderate oven about 40 minutes or until peppers are tender. Serve peppers with tomato sauce and a mixed green salad, if desired.

TOMATO SAUCE Heat oil in large deep flameproof baking dish; cook garlic, onion, cumin and oregano, stirring, until onion softens. Add undrained tomatoes and the water; bring to a boil. Reduce heat; simmer, uncovered, 10 minutes.

SERVES 4
PER SERVING 43.8g FAT; 2725KJ (652 CAL)

■ This recipe is our version of the classic Mexican 'chiles rellenos', stuffed Anaheim peppers. We used romano peppers also known as Hungarian peppers, banana chillies or sweet banana peppers, which are almost as mild as a normal pepper but also possess a slightly sweet sharp taste. Sold in varying degrees of ripeness, they are available in pale olive green, yellow, orange and red.

red lentil & vegetable stew

4 MEDIUM COURGETTES (480g)
4 SMALL AUBERGINES (240g)
1 MEDIUM RED PEPPER (200g)
2 TABLESPOONS OLIVE OIL
2 CLOVES GARLIC, CRUSHED
1 MEDIUM LEEK (350g), SLICED THINLY
1 TEASPOON CARAWAY SEEDS
1 TEASPOON CUMIN SEEDS
2 X 425g CANS TOMATOES
80ml DRY RED WINE
1 TEASPOON BROWN SUGAR
60ml TOMATO PASTE
200g RED LENTILS
500ml VEGETABLE STOCK
1 TABLESPOON FINELY CHOPPED FRESH BASIL

PREPARATION TIME 25 MINUTES   **COOKING TIME** 45 MINUTES

1   Halve courgettes and aubergines lengthways. Quarter pepper; remove seeds and membranes.
2   Heat 1 tablespoon of the oil heated grill plate (or grill or barbecue); cook vegetables, in batches, until browned on both sides. Remove from pan.
3   Heat remaining oil in large saucepan; cook garlic, leek and seeds, stirring, until leek is soft. Add undrained crushed tomatoes, wine, sugar, paste and lentils; simmer, uncovered, 5 minutes.
4   Stir in stock, basil and vegetables; simmer, uncovered, about 15 minutes or until vegetables are tender.

SERVES 4
PER SERVING   13.6g FAT; 1215KJ (290 CAL)

vegetarian

potato & sweet potato curry

2 TABLESPOONS VEGETABLE OIL
1 TEASPOON FENUGREEK SEEDS
1 TEASPOON GROUND CUMIN
1 TEASPOON GROUND CORIANDER
1 TEASPOON GARAM MASALA
1/2 TEASPOON GROUND TURMERIC
2 CLOVES GARLIC, CRUSHED
1 LONG GREEN CHILLI, SLICED THINLY
700g POTATOES, CHOPPED COARSELY
1 LARGE SWEET POTATO (500g), CHOPPED COARSELY
2 X 400g CAN CRUSHED TOMATOES
250ml VEGETABLE STOCK
70g PLAIN YOGURT
2 LARGE BROWN ONIONS (400g), SLICED THINLY
30g LOOSELY PACKED FRESH CORIANDER LEAVES

PREPARATION TIME 20 MINUTES COOKING TIME 1 HOUR 25 MINUTES

1 Heat half of the oil in large saucepan; cook spices, garlic and chilli, stirring, until fragrant. Add potato and sweet potato; cook, stirring, 5 minutes.
2 Stir in undrained tomatoes and stock; bring to a boil. Reduce heat; simmer, covered, about 1 hour or until potato and sweet potato are tender. Stir in yogurt.
3 Meanwhile, heat remaining oil in medium frying pan; cook onion, stirring, until onion browns lightly.
4 Divide curry among serving plates; top with onion and coriander. Serve with steamed basmati rice, if desired.

SERVES 4
PER SERVING 10.8g FAT; 1342KJ (321 CAL)

vegetarian

roasted root vegetable ratatouille

PREPARATION TIME 40 MINUTES   COOKING TIME 1 HOUR 30 MINUTES

800g CELERIAC, TRIMMED, CHOPPED COARSELY
2 LARGE CARROTS (360g), CHOPPED COARSELY
2 MEDIUM PARSNIPS (500g), CHOPPED COARSELY
2 MEDIUM SWEET POTATOES (800g), CHOPPED COARSELY
80ml OLIVE OIL
1 LARGE BROWN ONION (200g), CHOPPED FINELY
3 CLOVES GARLIC, CRUSHED
3 TABLESPOONS LOOSELY PACKED FRESH OREGANO LEAVES
1 TABLESPOON TOMATO PASTE
2 X 425g CANS CRUSHED TOMATOES
125ml DRY RED WINE
250ml WATER
40g COARSELY GRATED PARMESAN CHEESE
250g COARSELY GRATED MOZZARELLA CHEESE
70g FRESH BREADCRUMBS
2 TEASPOONS FINELY GRATED LEMON RIND
30g COARSELY CHOPPED FRESH FLAT-LEAF PARSLEY
2 TABLESPOONS COARSELY CHOPPED FRESH OREGANO

1 Preheat oven to hot.
2 Combine celeriac, carrot, parsnip, sweet potato and half of the oil in large deep baking dish. Roast, uncovered, in hot oven about 50 minutes or until vegetables are tender and browned lightly, stirring halfway through cooking time.
3 Meanwhile, heat remaining oil in large saucepan; cook onion, garlic and oregano leaves, stirring, until onion softens. Add paste; cook, stirring, 1 minute. Add undrained tomatoes, wine and the water; bring to a boil. Boil, uncovered, 10 minutes.
4 Add tomato mixture to vegetables in dish; toss gently to combine. Sprinkle with combined cheeses, breadcrumbs, rind, parsley and chopped oregano. Cook, uncovered, in hot oven about 20 minutes or until top browns lightly. Serve with a lemon vinaigrette-dressed green leafy salad, if desired.

SERVES 6
PER SERVING 24.7g FAT; 2090KJ (500 CAL)

CELERIAC, a member of the celery family, is a tuberous brown-skinned root having a white flesh that tastes like a very earthy, more pungent celery. Sometimes called knob celery, celeriac is the cooking celery of Northern Europe. Peeled and diced, it can be used raw in salads or on a crudités platter; steamed or boiled, it can be mashed like potato or diced and served as a cooked vegetable.

vindaloo vegetables

PREPARATION TIME 25 MINUTES
COOKING TIME 50 MINUTES

1 TABLESPOON VEGETABLE OIL
2 MEDIUM BROWN ONIONS (300g), CHOPPED COARSELY
2 CLOVES GARLIC, CRUSHED
60ml VINDALOO CURRY PASTE
12 BABY NEW POTATOES (480g)
800g BUTTERNUT SQUASH, CHOPPED COARSELY
1 LARGE RED PEPPER (350g), CHOPPED COARSELY
3 MEDIUM CARROTS (360g), CHOPPED COARSELY
1/4 MEDIUM CAULIFLOWER (400g), CHOPPED COARSELY
375ml VEGETABLE STOCK
425ml CAN COCONUT MILK
2 DRIED LIME LEAVES
50g CURRANTS
3 FRESH TRIMMED CORN COBS (750g), CHOPPED COARSELY
3 MEDIUM COURGETTES (350g), CHOPPED COARSELY
400g BROCCOLI, CHOPPED COARSELY
35g CHOPPED ROASTED UNSALTED PEANUTS

1 Heat oil in large saucepan; cook onion and garlic, stirring, until onion is soft. Add curry paste; cook, stirring, until fragrant.
2 Add potatoes, squash, pepper, carrot, cauliflower, stock, coconut milk, lime leaves and currants; simmer, covered, 20 minutes.
3 Stir in corn, courgettes and broccoli; simmer, covered, about 20 minutes or until vegetables are tender.
4 Serve sprinkled with peanuts.

SERVES 4
PER SERVING 36.5g FAT; 3422KJ (817 CAL)

STORAGE Recipe can be made a day ahead and refrigerated, covered. Recipe suitable for freezing.

grilled aubergines with chickpeas

PREPARATION TIME 20 MINUTES
COOKING TIME 1 HOUR

2 MEDIUM AUBERGINES (600g), SLICED THICKLY
2 TABLESPOONS OLIVE OIL
10 SPRING ONIONS (250g), TRIMMED
2 CLOVES GARLIC, CRUSHED
3 TRIMMED STICKS CELERY (225g), SLICED THINLY
2 X 310g CANS CHICKPEAS, RINSED, DRAINED
4 LARGE TOMATOES (1kg), PEELED, CHOPPED FINELY
15g FINELY CHOPPED FRESH PARSLEY
15g FINELY CHOPPED FRESH OREGANO
1 TABLESPOON TOMATO PASTE
150g ITALIAN BEANS, TRIMMED, HALVED

1   Place aubergine slices on greased oven tray; brush lightly with about half of the oil. Grill until browned on both sides.
2   Heat remaining oil in 3 litre flameproof casserole dish; cook onion, stirring, until onion is browned lightly.
3   Stir in aubergine, garlic, celery, chickpeas, tomato and herbs. Cook, covered, in moderate oven about 45 minutes or until vegetables are tender.
4   Remove from oven; stir in tomato paste and beans.

SERVES 4
PER SERVING 12.4g FAT; 1128KJ (269 CAL)

potato & cheese kofta with tomato tamarind sauce

PREPARATION TIME 30 MINUTES (PLUS STANDING TIME)
COOKING TIME 35 MINUTES

2 MEDIUM POTATOES (400g)
2 TABLESPOONS FINELY CHOPPED FRESH CORIANDER
75g TOASTED UNSALTED CASHEWS, CHOPPED FINELY
60g FROZEN PEAS, THAWED
VEGETABLE OIL, FOR DEEP-FRYING
4 HARD-BOILED EGGS, HALVED

CHEESE
1 LITRE MILK
2 TABLESPOONS LEMON JUICE

TOMATO TAMARIND SAUCE
1 TABLESPOON OLIVE OIL
1 CLOVE GARLIC, CRUSHED
3cm (1in) PIECE FRESH GINGER (15g), GRATED
$^1/_2$ TEASPOON DRIED CHILLI FLAKES
1 TEASPOON GROUND CUMIN
1 TEASPOON GROUND CORIANDER
$^1/_2$ TEASPOON MUSTARD SEEDS
60ml TAMARIND CONCENTRATE
2 X 400g CANS CRUSHED TOMATOES

1 Make cheese. Make tomato tamarind sauce.
2 Meanwhile, boil, steam or microwave potato until tender; drain.
3 Mash potato in large bowl; stir in cheese, coriander, nuts and peas. Heat oil in wok; deep-fry level tablespoons of the potato mixture, in batches, until cooked through. Drain on absorbent paper.
4 Add koftas to tomato tamarind sauce; simmer, uncovered, 5 minutes. Divide koftas and sauce among serving plates; top with egg.

CHEESE Bring milk to a boil in medium saucepan. Remove from heat; stir in juice. Cool 10 minutes. Pour through muslin-lined sieve into medium bowl; stand cheese mixture in sieve over bowl for 40 minutes. Discard liquid in bowl.

TOMATO TAMARIND SAUCE Heat oil in large saucepan; cook garlic and ginger, stirring, until fragrant. Add chilli, spices and seeds; cook, stirring, 1 minute. Add tamarind and undrained tomatoes; bring to a boil. Reduce heat; simmer, uncovered, 5 minutes.

SERVES 4
PER SERVING 29.7g FAT; 2144KJ (513 CAL)

TAMARIND is associated with the food of India and South-East Asia, but is actually the product of a native tropical African tree that grows as high as 25 metres. The tree produces clusters of brown "hairy" pods, each of which is filled with seeds and a viscous pulp that are dried and pressed into the blocks of tamarind found in Asian supermarkets.

side dishes

mashed potato variations

LEEK AND THYME

PREPARATION TIME 20 MINUTES COOKING TIME 25 MINUTES

I TABLESPOON VEGETABLE OIL
I SMALL LEEK (200g), SLICED THINLY
I CLOVE GARLIC, CRUSHED
I TABLESPOON FINELY CHOPPED FRESH THYME
2 TABLESPOONS DRY WHITE WINE

Heat oil in large saucepan; cook leek, garlic and thyme, stirring, until leek is soft. Add wine; cook, stirring, until wine evaporates. Stir leek mixture into basic mashed potato.

SERVES 4 PER SERVING 13.7g FAT; 1144KJ (273 CAL)

THAI-STYLE

PREPARATION TIME 20 MINUTES COOKING TIME 25 MINUTES

60ml COCONUT CREAM
I TABLESPOON VEGETABLE OIL
I SMALL BROWN ONION (80g), CHOPPED FINELY
I CLOVE GARLIC, CRUSHED
I SMALL FRESH RED CHILLI, DESEEDED, CHOPPED FINELY
I TEASPOON GRATED FRESH GINGER
I TABLESPOON FINELY CHOPPED FRESH CORIANDER

Substitute coconut cream for milk in basic mashed potato recipe. Heat oil in large saucepan; cook onion, garlic, chilli and ginger, stirring, until onion is soft. Add to mashed potato with coriander; mix well.

SERVES 4 PER SERVING 16.8g FAT; 1241KJ (296 CAL)

BASIC MASHED POTATO

PREPARATION TIME
15 MINUTES COOKING
TIME 20 MINUTES

4 MEDIUM OLD POTATOES (800g)
40g BUTTER
60ml MILK
I TEASPOON BROWN SUGAR

I Peel potatoes; cut each into four even pieces. Boil, steam or microwave potatoes until tender; drain. Mash well using potato masher or fork, or push potato through sieve.
2 Add butter, milk and sugar, beat until butter melts.

STORAGE Basic recipe and variations best made just before serving.

PINE NUT

PREPARATION TIME 15 MINUTES
COOKING TIME 25 MINUTES

50g PINE NUTS, TOASTED
2 TEASPOONS FINELY CHOPPED FRESH ROSEMARY

Add pine nuts and rosemary to basic mashed
potato; mix well.

SERVES 4
PER SERVING 17.8g FAT; 1271K (304 CAL)

BACON & MUSTARD

PREPARATION TIME 20 MINUTES
COOKING TIME 25 MINUTES

4 BACON RASHERS (285g), CHOPPED FINELY
3 TEASPOONS WHOLEGRAIN MUSTARD
1 TABLESPOON FINELY CHOPPED FRESH PARSLEY

Cook bacon in large frying pan until crisp; drain
on absorbent paper. Add bacon, mustard and
parsley to basic mashed potato; mix well.

SERVES 4
PER SERVING 12.3g FAT; 1170KJ (279 CAL)

CAJUN

PREPARATION TIME 25 MINUTES
COOKING TIME 30 MINUTES

1 SMALL RED PEPPER (150g), ROASTED, SLICED THINLY
½ TEASPOON CAJUN SEASONING
1 TEASPOON FINELY CHOPPED FRESH THYME

Add pepper, spice mix and thyme to basic
mashed potato; mix well.

SERVES 4
PER SERVING 9.1g FAT; 947KJ (226 CAL)

ITALIAN

PREPARATION TIME 20 MINUTES
COOKING TIME 20 MINUTES

20g GRATED PARMESAN CHEESE
40g SLICED PITTED BLACK OLIVES
1 TABLESPOON FINELY CHOPPED FRESH BASIL

Add cheese, olives and basil to mashed potato;
mix well.

SERVES 4
PER SERVING 10.7g FAT; 1046KJ (250 CAL)

FETA & BLACK OLIVE MASH

Boil, steam or microwave 1kg coarsely chopped potato until tender; drain. Mash potato in large bowl with 1 tablespoon olive oil until smooth. Stir in 165ml warmed buttermilk, 200g finely chopped feta and 60g thinly sliced black olives. Drizzle with another tablespoon of olive oil.

CREAMY GARLIC MASH

Place 1kg coarsely chopped potato, 750ml milk and 1 peeled garlic clove in medium saucepan; bring to a boil. Reduce heat; simmer, partially covered, about 15 minutes or until potato is soft. Discard garlic. Strain potato over medium jug; reserve 165ml of the milk. Transfer potato to large bowl; mash with reserved milk and 40g of softened butter until smooth.

ROASTED SWEET POTATO PUREE

Cut 1 large sweet potato into 4cm (1½in) chunks and place on a baking tray. Cover and bake in moderately hot oven about 50 minutes or until tender. Blend or process the sweet potato with 165ml whipping cream, ¼ teaspoon ground cumin and ¼ teaspoon mixed spice until smooth.

PARSNIP MASH

Boil, steam or microwave 1kg coarsely chopped parsnip until tender; drain. Mash parsnip in medium bowl with 190ml hot milk until smooth; stir in 2 crushed cloves garlic and 40g softened butter.

SOFT POLENTA

Combine 750ml water and 500ml vegetable stock in large saucepan; bring to a boil. Gradually add 340g polenta to liquid, stirring constantly. Reduce heat; simmer, stirring, about 10 minutes or until polenta thickens. Add 250ml milk and 3 tablespoons finely grated parmesan cheese; stir until cheese melts.

CHEESY POLENTA

Combine 580ml water and 580ml milk in large saucepan; bring to a boil. Gradually add 170g polenta to liquid, stirring constantly. Reduce heat; simmer, stirring, about 10 minutes or until polenta thickens. Stir in 35g finely grated parmesan cheese and 30g butter.

ROAST POTATOES

Preheat oven to hot. Lightly oil oven tray. Boil, steam or microwave 6 halved medium potatoes 5 minutes; drain. Pat dry with absorbent paper; cool 10 minutes. Gently rake rounded sides of potatoes with tines of fork; place potato in single layer, cut-side down, on prepared oven tray. Brush with 2 tablespoons olive oil; roast, uncovered, in hot oven about 50 minutes or until potatoes are browned lightly and crisp.

BALSAMIC-ROASTED POTATOES

Combine 1kg halved small potatoes, 30g melted butter and 2 tablespoons balsamic vinegar in medium baking dish. Roast, uncovered, in moderately slow oven about 1¼ hours or until potatoes are tender and browned lightly, brushing potatoes occasionally with vinegar mixture in dish.

SAFFRON COUSCOUS

Boil 500ml chicken stock in large saucepan with pinch ground saffron. Remove from heat; stir in 380g couscous. Stand 5 minutes; fluff using fork. Heat 40g butter in pan. Add couscous; cook, stirring, until combined.

SPINACH COUSCOUS

Combine 285g couscous with 375ml boiling water in large heat-proof bowl, cover; stand for about 5 minutes or until water is absorbed, fluffing with fork occasionally. Stir in 80g finely shredded baby spinach leaves.

OLIVE & PARSLEY COUSCOUS

Bring 375ml vegetable stock to a boil in medium saucepan. Remove from heat; stir in 285g couscous and 30g butter. Cover; stand about 5 minutes or until liquid is absorbed, fluffing with fork occasionally. Stir in 120g pitted kalamata olives and 30g chopped fresh flat-leaf parsley.

CUMIN COUSCOUS

Combine 250ml boiling water and 190g couscous in medium heat-proof bowl, cover; stand about 5 minutes or until liquid is absorbed, fluffing occasionally with a fork. Add 1 tablespoon olive oil and 1 teaspoon ground cumin; toss gently to combine. Sprinkle with a thinly sliced spring onion.

SPANISH RICE & PEAS

Combine 750ml of water and 65ml olive oil in medium saucepan; bring to a boil. Stir in 400g medium-grain white rice and cook, uncovered, without stirring, for about 10 minutes or until liquid has almost evaporated. Reduce heat; simmer, covered, 5 minutes. Gently stir in 120g frozen peas and simmer, covered, for about 5 minutes or until rice and peas are tender.

PILAF

Melt 20g butter in medium saucepan; cook 1 clove crushed garlic, stirring, until fragrant. Add 200g basmati rice; cook, stirring, 1 minute. Add 250ml chicken stock and 250ml water; bring to a boil. Reduce heat; simmer, covered, about 20 minutes or until rice is just tender. Remove from heat; fluff rice with fork. Stir in 3 tablespoons coarsely chopped fresh flat-leaf parsley and 20g toasted flaked almonds.

ROASTED CORN SALSA

Roast 3 husked corn cobs on heated oiled grill plate (or grill or barbecue) until browned all over. When corn is cool enough to handle, cut kernels from cobs. Combine corn kernels in medium bowl with 1 coarsely chopped small red onion, 1 coarsely chopped medium avocado, 250g halved cherry tomatoes, 2 tablespoons lime juice and 3 tablespoons chopped fresh coriander.

MUSTARD & HONEY-GLAZED ROAST SWEET POTATOES

Halve 2.5kg unpeeled sweet potatoes lengthways; cut each half into 2cm (¾in) wedges. Combine 230g honey, 90G wholegrain mustard and 2 tablespoons coarsely chopped fresh rosemary in large bowl. Toss sweet potatoes in mixture. Divide sweet potatoes between two large shallow baking dishes. Roast, uncovered, in hot oven about 1 hour or until sweet potatoes are tender and slightly caramelised. (Serves 8.)

side dishes

TOMATO & RED ONION SALAD

Arrange 4 thinly sliced medium tomatoes and 2 thinly sliced medium red onions on serving platter; drizzle with 2 tablespoons red wine vinegar and 1 tablespoon olive oil. Sprinkle with cracked black pepper.

TOMATO & HERB SALAD

Place 5 coarsely chopped medium tomatoes, 2 tablespoons chopped fresh mint, 3 tablespoons chopped fresh flat-leaf parsley and 2 tablespoons chopped fresh dill in medium bowl. Place 2 cloves crushed garlic, 2 tablespoons lemon juice, 1 tablespoon olive oil and 2 teaspoons white vinegar in screw-top jar; shake well. Drizzle dressing over salad; toss to combine.

PARMESAN & BABY SPINACH SALAD

Place 100g baby spinach leaves, 50g shaved parmesan cheese and 1 tablespoon toasted pine nuts in large bowl. Combine 2 table-spoons balsamic vinegar and 1 tablespoon olive oil in screw-top jar; shake well. Drizzle dressing over salad; toss gently to combine.

CUCUMBER RAITA

Served with meat curries such as this rogan josh, raita not only introduces different flavours to a meal but also tempers the spiciness of the dish. Combine 280g thick 'country-style' yogurt, 1 finely chopped cucumber and 1 tablespoon finely chopped fresh mint in a small bowl with salt, pepper and ground cumin to taste.

side dishes

glossary

ALLSPICE also known as pimento or jamaican pepper; so-named because it tastes like a combination of nutmeg, cumin, clove and cinnamon – all spices.
ALMONDS flat, pointy ended nuts with pitted brown shell enclosing a creamy white kernel that is covered by a brown skin.
BLANCHED skins removed.
FLAKED paper-thin slices.
SLIVERED cut lengthways.
ARTICHOKE, GLOBE large flower head of a plant from the thistle family.
AUBERGINE eggplant.
BARLEY a nutritious grain used in soups and stews as well as in whiskey- and beer-making.
BAY LEAVES aromatic leaves from the bay tree.
BEANS
BLACK-EYED also known as black-eyed peas.
BORLOTTI (roman beans); pale pink with darker red spots, eaten fresh or dried.
BROAD (fava beans) available fresh, canned or frozen. Fresh are best peeled twice, discarding both the outer long green pod and the sandy-green tough inner shell.
GREEN sometimes called french beans.
HARICOT small, dried white bean similar in appearance and flavour to navy and canneloni beans.
RED KIDNEY have a floury texture and fairly sweet flavour; colour can vary from pink to maroon.
BEEF any cuts of beef suitable for stewing are also suitable for casseroles; including blade steak and chuck steak, as listed here, plus gravy beef, rib steak and skirt steak.

BLADE STEAK a cut from the shoulder blade area.
BRISKET from the under section of the forequarter and ribs, rolled and secured with string or netting.
CHUCK STEAK from the neck area; can be used as one piece or as steak.
SPARE RIBS we used the shorter spare ribs which are quite lean but meaty; these are also known as baby back ribs.
BREADCRUMBS packaged fine-textured, crunchy, purchased, white breadcrumbs. stale one- or two-day-old bread made into crumbs by blending or processing.
BRANDY spirit distilled from wine. breadcrumbs, stale use 1- or 2-day-old bread made into crumbs by grating, blending or processing.
BROCCOLINI a cross between broccoli and chinese kale. Is milder and sweeter than broccoli.
BUTTER use salted or unsalted (sweet) butter; 125g is equal to one stick butter.
CAJUN SEASONING combination of dried ingredients consisting of salt, peppers, garlic, onion and spices.
CAPERS pickled buds of a Mediterranean shrub.
CARAWAY SEEDS a member of the parsley family; available in seed or ground form and can be used in sweet and savoury dishes.
CARDAMOM native to India and purchased in pod, seed or ground form; has a distinctive aromatic, sweetly rich flavour.
CAYENNE PEPPER a thin-fleshed, long, extremely hot red chilli; usually purchased dried and ground.
celeriac tuberous root with brown skin, white flesh and a celery-like flavour.

CELERIAC tuberous root with brown skin, white flesh and celery-like flavour.
CHEESE
BOCCONCINI small balls of mild, delicate cheese packaged in water or whey to keep them white and soft; any yellowing indicates they are old.
PARMESAN sharp-tasting hard cheese used as a flavour accent. We use fresh parmesan cheese, although it is available already finely grated.
CHICKEN
BREAST with skin and bone intact.
BREAST FILLET no skin and bones.
DRUMSTICK leg with skin intact.
LEG JOINT leg and thigh with skin intact.
THIGH has skin and bone intact.
THIGH FILLET no skin and bones.
CHICKPEAS (garbanzos) an irregularly round, sandy coloured legume.
CHILLIES available in many different types and sizes. Use rubber gloves when chopping fresh chillies as they can burn your skin. Removing seeds and membranes lessens the heat level.
CHIPOTLE a dried, smoked jalapeño chilli. It has a deep, intensely smokey flavour, rather than a searing heat. They are dark brown in appearance. Available in cans. flakes crushed, dried chillies.
GREEN these are generally unripened thai chillies, but sometimes varieties that are ripe when green, such as habanero, poblano or serrano chillies are used.
THAI RED small, bright red with a medium heat.
CINNAMON STICK dried inner bark of the shoots of the cinnamon tree.

COCONUT

CREAM the first pressing from grated mature coconut flesh.

MILK the second pressing (less rich) from grated mature coconut flesh.

COURGETTE zucchini.

COUSCOUS a fine cereal made from semolina.

CREAM fresh pouring cream; has a minimum fat content of 35 per cent.

SOUR a thick commercially cultured soured cream

WHIPPING has a minimum fat content of 35 per cent; and includes a thickener.

DASHI basic fish and seaweed stock made from dried bonito (a type of fish) flakes and kelp (kombu). Available from Asian specialty stores.

FENNEL has a slight aniseed taste when fresh, ground or in seed form. The bulb can be eaten uncooked in salads or braised, steamed or stir-fried.

FISH SAUCE made from the liquid drained from salted, fermented anchovies. Has a strong smell and taste; use sparingly. Several varieties are available and the intensity of flavour varies. We used thai fish sauce.

FIVE SPICE POWDER a pungent mixture of ground spices including cinnamon, cloves, fennel, star anise and sichuan peppers.

FLOUR, WHITE PLAIN all-purpose flour.

GAI LARN also known as kanah, gai lum, Chinese broccoli and chinese kale; appreciated more for its stems than its coarse leaves. Can be steamed and stir-fried.

GALANGAL also known as ka, a rhizome with a hot ginger-citrusy flavour; used similarly to ginger and garlic. Fresh ginger can be substituted, but the flavour of the dish will not be the same.

GARAM MASALA a blend of cardamom, cinnamon, cloves, coriander, fennel and cumin.

GINGER also known as green or root ginger.

GROUND powdered ginger; cannot be substituted for fresh ginger.

GHEE a pure butter fat; it can be heated to high temperatures without burning because of the lack of salts and milk solids.

HERBS we have specified when to use fresh or dried herbs. If substituting dried herbs for fresh, use dried (not ground) herbs in the proportions of 1:4, e.g., 1 teaspoon dried herbs instead of 4 teaspoons (1 tablespoon) chopped fresh herbs.

ITALIAN SAUSAGES large fresh pork sausages, salted lightly.

JALAPENO PEPPERS hot chillies, available in brine in bottles and cans. jam a preserve of sugar and fruit.

JUNIPER BERRIES aromatic flavour; an ingredient of gin.

KAFFIR LIME LEAVES looks like two glossy dark green leaves joined end to end, forming a rounded hourglass shape. Sold fresh, dried or frozen. A strip of fresh lime peel can be substituted for each kaffir lime leaf.

KALONJI also known as nigella or black onion seeds; are angular seeds, black on the outside and creamy within, having a sharp nutty flavour.

LAMB any cuts of lamb suitable for stewing are also suitable for casseroles.

CHUMP CHOP the chump is the cut from just above the hind legs to the mid-loin section; it can be used as a piece for roasting, or cut into chops.

CUTLET small, tender rib chop.

DICED cubed lean meat.

LEG from the hindquarter.

NECK CHOP we used 'best' neck chops.

RACK row of cutlets.

ROLLED SHOULDER boneless section of the forequarter, rolled and secured with string or netting.

SHANK forequarter leg.

LARD fat obtained from melting down and clarifying pork fat; available packaged.

LEEK a member of the onion family; resembles the spring onion, but is much larger.

LEMONGRASS lemon-tasting, sharp edged grass; The white lower stem is used. Strips of lemon zest can be substituted.

LENTILS many different varieties of dried legumes; often identified by and named after their colour.

MADEIRA wine fortified with brandy.

MANGETOUT (eat all) also known as. snow peas.

MIRIN is a Japanese, champagne-coloured, cooking wine; should not be confused with sake.

MIXED SPICE a blend of ground spices, consisting of cinnamon, allspice and nutmeg.

MUSHROOMS

BUTTON small, cultivated white mushrooms having a delicate, subtle flavour.

CHESTNUT light to dark brown mushrooms with full-bodied flavour. Button or cup mushrooms can be substituted.

FLAT large, soft, flat mushrooms with a rich earthy flavour.

SHIITAKE (chinese black mushrooms) have a unique meaty flavour. Available fresh and dried.

MUSSELS should be bought from a fish market, fresh and closed tightly. Before cooking, scrub shells with a strong brush to remove the 'beards'. Discard any shells that do not open after cooking.

MUSTARD

FRENCH plain mild mustard.

SEEDED (wholegrain) a French-style coarse-grain mustard made from mustard seeds and dijon-style french mustard.

NAAN leavened bread associated with tandoori dishes of northern India.

NUTMEG the dried nut of an evergreen tree native to Indonesia; also available in ground form.

OIL

OLIVE a blend of refined and virgin olive oils, good for everyday cooking.

PEANUT made from ground peanuts, is the most commonly-used oil in Asian cooking; however, a lighter, salad type of oil can be used.

VEGETABLE we used a polyunsaturated vegetable oil.

OKRA also known as bamia or lady fingers; a green ridged, oblong pod with furry skin.

ONION

RED large purplish-red onion.

SPRING have crisp, narrow green-leafed tops and a fairly large sweet white bulb.

PAK CHOY (bok choy or chinese white cabbage) has a fresh, mild mustard taste and is good braised or in stir-fries. Baby pak choy is also available.

PANCETTA cured pork belly; bacon can be substituted.

PAPRIKA ground dried red pepper; available sweet or hot.

PARSNIP root vegetable shaped like a carrot; has a herb-like flavour.

PEANUT BUTTER peanuts ground to a paste; available in crunchy and smooth varieties.

PEPPER (capsicum or bell pepper) seeds and membrane should be discarded before use.

POLENTA also known as cornmeal; a flour-like cereal made of dried corn (maize) sold ground in several different textures.

PORK any cuts of pork suitable for stewing are also suitable for casseroles.

FOREQUARTER CHOPS from the shoulder area.

NECK boneless cut.

PORT a rich, sweet dessert wine fortified with brandy.

PRAWNS shrimp.

PROSCIUTTO uncooked, un-smoked, cured ham; ready to eat when bought.

PRUNES whole dried plums.

PUFF PASTRY, READY-ROLLED frozen sheets of puff pastry.

RICE

BASMATI a white, fragrant long-grained rice; should be washed several times before cooking.

JASMINE aromatic long-grain white rice.

LONG-GRAIN elongated grain, remains separate when cooked.

SAFFRON available in strands or ground form; imparts a yellow-orange colour to food. Store in the freezer.

SAKE Japan's favourite rice wine. If sake is unavailable, dry sherry, vermouth or brandy can be used as a substitute.

SAMBAL OELEK (ulek or olek) a salty paste made from ground chillies.

SAUCES

HOISIN a thick, sweet and spicy Chinese paste made from salted fermented soy beans, onions and garlic.

KECAP MANIS a dark, thick, sweet soy sauce

SOY also known as sieu; made from fermented soy beans.

SCALLOPS we used the scallops with coral (roe) attached.

SEASONED PEPPER a combination of black pepper, sugar and bell pepper.

SESAME SEEDS there are two types, black and white; we used the white variety. To toast, spread seeds evenly onto oven tray, toast in moderate oven for about 5 minutes or stir over heat in heavy-based pan until golden brown.

SHALLOTS also called french shallots, golden shallots or eschalots; small, elongated, brown-skinned members of the onion family.

SHERRY fortified wine consumed as an apertif or used in cooking. Sold as fino (light, dry), amontillado (medium sweet, dark) and oloroso (full-bodied, very dark).

SICHUAN PEPPERCORNS a mildly hot spice also known as szechuan or chinese pepper. Have a distinctive peppery-lemon flavour and aroma.

SPINACH a soft-leafed vegetable, with a delicate taste.

STAR ANISE the dried star-shaped fruit of an evergreen tree. It is used sparingly in Chinese cooking and has an aniseed flavour.

STOCK 250ml stock is equivalent to 250ml water plus 1 crumbled stock cube (or 1 teaspoon crumbled stock powder).

SUGAR we used coarse granulated table sugar, also known as crystal sugar, unless otherwise specified.

BROWN a soft fine granulated sugar containing molasses.

PALM (gula jawa, gula melaka and jaggery) fine sugar from the coconut palm; sold in cakes. Brown or black sugar can be substituted.

SWEDE a type of turnip; also as rutabaga.

SWEET POTATO fleshy orange root vegetable.

TAMARIND SAUCE if unavailable, soak about 30g dried tamarind in a cup of hot water, stand 10 minutes, squeeze pulp as dry as possible and use the flavoured water.

TOMATO

PASTE a concentrated tomato puree used for flavouring.

PUREE canned pureed tomatoes (not tomato paste). Fresh, peeled, pureed tomatoes may be substituted.

SUN-DRIED (de-hydrated tomatoes) we used sun-dried tomatoes packaged in oil, unless otherwise specified.

SUMAC a purple-red, astringent spice that adds a tart, lemony flavour. Can be found in Middle-Eastern food stores.

TAMARIND CONCENTRATE (or paste) the distillation of tamarind juice into a condensed, compacted paste. Thick and purple-black, it is ready-to-use, with no soaking or straining.

TURMERIC a member of the ginger family; its root is dried and ground. It is intensely pungent in taste, but not hot.

UDON NOODLES available fresh and dried, these Japanese broad white wheat noodles are similar to the ones in homemade chicken noodle soup.

VEAL the meat from a very young calf; identified by its pale pink flesh.

CUTLET choice chop from the mid-loin (back) area.

DICED cubed lean meat.

FOREQUARTER area containing neck, shoulder and ribs.

OSSO BUCCO this famous Italian dish used the hind or forequarter shank or knuckle cut into medallions. When the knuckle is trimmed of meat at the thin end, this is known as a 'Frenched' knuckle.

SHOULDER from the forequarter.

STEAK schnitzel.

VINEGAR

BALSAMIC originated in the province of Modena, Italy. Regional wine is specially processed then aged in antique wooden casks to give a pungent flavour.

BROWN MALT made from fermented malt and beech shavings.

WHITE made from spirit of cane sugar.

WHITE WINE made from white wine.

WORCESTERSHIRE SAUCE a thin, dark-brown spicy sauce used as a seasoning for meat, gravies and cocktails and as a condiment.

index

conversion charts

MEASURES

■ The spoon measurements used in this book are metric: one metric tablespoon holds 20ml; one metric teaspoon holds 5ml.

■ All spoon measurements are level.

■ The most accurate way of measuring dry ingredients is to weigh them.

■ When measuring liquids, use a clear glass or plastic jug with metric markings.

■ We use large eggs with an average weight of 60g.

DRY MEASURES

metric	imperial
15g	$^1/_2$oz
30g	1oz
60g	2oz
90g	3oz
125g	4oz ($^1/_4$lb)
155g	5oz
185g	6oz
220g	7oz
250g	8oz ($^1/_2$lb)
280g	9oz
315g	10oz
345g	11oz
375g	12oz ($^3/_4$lb)
410g	13oz
440g	14oz
470g	15oz
500g	16oz (1lb)
750g	24oz (1$^1/_2$lb)
1kg	32oz (2lb)

LIQUID MEASURES

metric	imperial
30ml	1 fl oz
60ml	2 fl oz
100ml	3 fl oz
125ml	4 fl oz
150ml	5 fl oz ($^1/_4$ pint/1 gill)
190ml	6 fl oz
250ml	8 fl oz
300ml	10 fl oz ($^1/_2$ pt)
500ml	16 fl oz
600ml	20 fl oz (1 pint)
1000ml (1 litre)	1$^3/_4$ pints

LENGTH MEASURES

metric	imperial
3mm	$^1/_8$in
6mm	$^1/_4$in
1cm	$^1/_2$in
2cm	$^3/_4$in
2.5cm	1in
5cm	2in
6cm	2$^1/_2$in
8cm	3in
10cm	4in
13cm	5in
15cm	6in
18cm	7in
20cm	8in
23cm	9in
25cm	10in
28cm	11in
30cm	12in (1ft)

OVEN TEMPERATURES

These oven temperatures are only a guide for conventional ovens. For fan-assisted ovens, check the manufacturer's manual.

	°C (Celcius)	°F (Fahrenheit)	gas mark
Very low	120	250	$^1/_2$
Low	150	275-300	1-2
Moderately low	170	325	3
Moderate	180	350-375	4-5
Moderately hot	200	400	6
Hot	220	425-450	7-8
Very hot	240	475	9